A STAB IN THE FRONT

THE SUEZ CONFLICT - 1956

by

SIR PHILIP GOODHART

First Published in Great Britain
by
WILTON 65
Hernes Keep, Winkfield, Windsor SL4 4SY
September 2006

ISBN 1-905060-06-8

AUTHOR

Sir Philip Goodhart landed at Port Said with the 1st Parachute Battalion on 6 November 1956. He entered the House of Commons in March 1957 after winning one of the first by-elections after the Suez campaign. Ten years earlier Sir Philip had served in Palestine with 1 Para and then joined the staff of 1st Parachute Brigade Headquarters (1945-1947).

After leaving the Army, Sir Philip read History at Trinity College, Cambridge where he edited Varsity, the undergraduate newspaper. While still an undergraduate he was the Conservative Candidate at the 1950 General Election for the coal-mining constituency of Consett, Co. Durham.

After leaving Cambridge, Sir Philip joined the Daily Telegraph and then the Sunday Times (1950-1956). He reported on President Eisenhower's first election campaign in 1952 and the Mau Mau revolt in Kenya. At Suez in 1956 he was the Sunday Times correspondent and went on to report from Israel after the cease fire.

In March 1957 Sir Philip won the by-election at Beckenham, a seat which he held for thirty-five years. For nineteen years (1960-1979) he was elected Secretary of the 1922 Committee. In Margaret Thatcher's first government he was a Minister at the Northern Ireland Office and at the Ministry of Defence.

Sir Philip's books include: *The Hunt for Kinathi,* an account of the end of the Mau Mau Campaign; *Fifty Ships that Saved the World* - the story of the destroyers-bases deal in 1940 which led to the Anglo-American military alliance; *Full Hearted Consent* - an account of the 1975 Euro Referendum and *1922* - the history of the first fifty years of the Committee. He worked with Sir Alistair Horne on his official biography of Harold Macmillan.

Sir Philip has a detailed knowledge of the political and military background to the Suez campaign. He has worked with many of those who played leading roles.

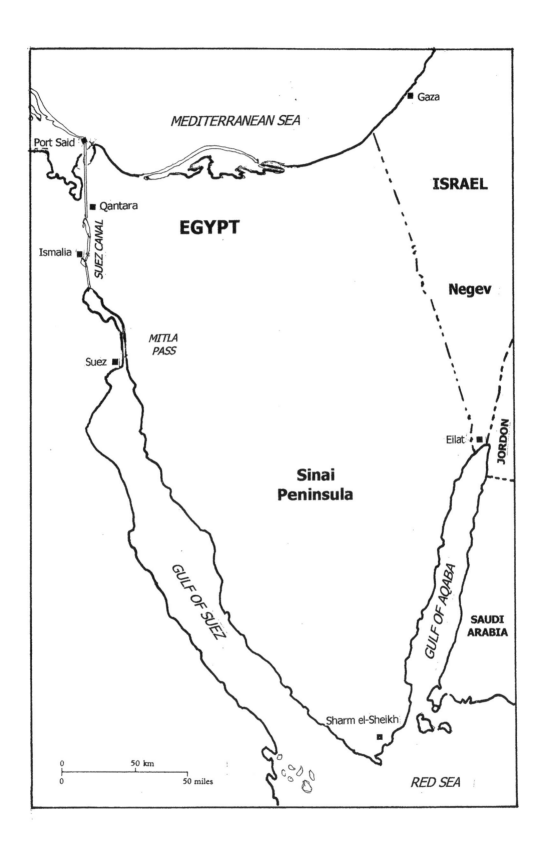

A STAB IN THE FRONT
The Suez Conflict, 1956

When he first heard that President Nasser of Egypt had nationalised the Suez Canal Company on July 26th 1956, Anthony Eden was giving a dinner party at 10 Downing Street. The guests of honour were King Faisal of Iraq and the Iraqi Prime Minister, Nuri es-Said. The Iraqi Prime Minister, who was Great Britain's senior political ally in the Middle East, immediately gave his host some belligerent advice: "Hit Nasser and hit him hard."

One of the other guests was Hugh Gaitskell, the Leader of the Opposition. According to his diary, Gaitskell asked Anthony Eden what he was going to do. The Prime Minister "thought perhaps they ought to take it to the Security Council ..... I said 'supposing Nasser doesn't take any notice?' Whereupon Selwyn (Lloyd, the Foreign Secretary) said: 'well ..... in that case an old-fashioned ultimatum will be necessary'. I said that I thought they ought to act quickly, whatever they did; and that as far as Great Britain was concerned, public opinion would almost certainly be behind them".

When the Cabinet met on the following morning there was a unanimous view that "strong and resolute action" should be taken. A Cabinet Committee of senior Ministers – the Egypt Committee – was set up to handle the crisis. The Daily Mirror's headline "Grabber Nasser" reflected the general view of the British press and the British public.

The national feeling of irritation and anger at Nasser's nationalisation was still flowing strongly when the House of Commons first debated the issue on August 2nd. The Prime Minister opened the debate by telling the House, "as the world is today, and as it is likely to be for some time to come, the industrial life of Western Europe literally depends upon the continuing free navigation of the Canal ..... Last year nearly 70 million tons of oil passed through the canal, representing about half the oil supplies of Western Europe. Traffic through the Canal moved at the rate of 40 ships a day and amounted to 154 million tons of shipping ..... nor does this traffic affect the West alone. Australia, India, Ceylon and a large part of South East Asia transport a large proportion of their trade through the Canal."

As Anthony Eden then noted, Nasser had announced that he was nationalising the Canal Company in order to pay for the construction of the Aswan Dam – a huge project that would control the floodwaters of the Nile. One week before Nasser's nationalisation, John Foster Dulles, the American Secretary of State, had announced the withdrawal of American financial support for the building of the dam, which was seen by many Egyptians as the potential cure for their country's economic problems. After pointing out that the revenue raised from charges on ships passing through the Canal could not possibly pay for the construction of the Aswan Dam, the Prime Minister turned his attention to the recent behaviour of President Nasser. "Is it possible for us to believe the word of the present Egyptian government to the extent of leaving it in their power alone to decide whether these supplies shall reach the Western World through the Canal? I truly think that we have done everything in our power to show our goodwill ..... Our reward has been broken faith and broken promises. We have been subjected to a ceaseless barrage of propaganda. This has been accompanied by intrigue and by attempts at subversion in British Territories." After telling the House that, "the action of the Egyptian government in compelling the Canal Company employees to remain at their posts under threat of imprisonment is certainly, to say the least, a violation of human rights", the Prime Minister went on to announce: "in view of the uncertain situation created by the actions of the Egyptian Government Her Majesty's Government have thought is necessary to take certain precautionary measures of a military nature. These measures include the movement from this country of certain Navy, Army and Airforce units and the recall of a limited number of Section A and AER Category 1 Reservists and also a limited number of Officers from the Regular Army Reserve of Officers."

When he spoke after the Prime Minister, Hugh Gaitskell, the Leader of the Opposition, added his own sharp criticism of President Nasser: "We cannot forget that Colonel Nasser has repeatedly boasted of his intention to create an Arab empire from the Atlantic to the Persian Gulf. The French Prime Minister, Monsieur Mollet, the other day quoted a speech of Colonel Nasser's and rightly said that it should remind us of only one thing – of the speeches of Hitler before the War. Colonel Nasser has certainly made a number of inflammatory speeches against us and his government has continually attempted subversion in Jordan and other Arab states. He has persistently threatened the State of Israel and made it plain, from time to time, that it is his purpose and intention to destroy Israel if he possibly can. That ..... is a clear enough notice of aggression."

The only note of equivocation came at the end of Hugh Gaitskell's speech: "We must not, therefore, allow ourselves to get into a position where we might be denounced in the Security Council as aggressors or where the majority of the Assembly was against us .....While force cannot be excluded we must be sure that the circumstances justify it and that it is, if used, consistent with our belief in, and our pledges to, the Charter of the United Nations and not in conflict with them."

There were even fewer cautionary passages in the speech of Herbert Morrison who had been Foreign Secretary in the last Labour government. He reminded the House of the similarity between "the customs of the former dictators of Italy and Germany and those of the modern dictator of Egypt". Herbert Morrison was also critical of the Americans: "If the United States will not stand with us, then we may have to stand without them."

Most of the back bench speeches from both sides of the House echoed the firm words of the Prime Minister and the Leader of the Opposition. There was a rumble of approval for Stanley Evans, the Labour Member of Parliament for Wednesbury, when he said: "there seems to be a basic unity in the House in its approach to this problem. I think that the growing claims of Nasser to be both Pope and Caesar to the entire Arab world is the poison in Middle Eastern affairs and that this Suez issue is a test of Western diplomatic and military solidarity."

The Joint Intelligence Committee Reports

On August 3rd, the day after the debate in the House of Commons, the Joint Intelligence Committee produced its first assessment of the impact of Nasser's action on the Middle East. The Joint Intelligence Committee brought together the heads of the Intelligence Services and senior representatives of the Foreign Office and Ministry of Defence. Its verdict was straightforward:"…..His nationalisation of the Canal has been a triumph."

The J.I.C. were particularly worried about the impact of Nasser's actions on the countries that had joined the Baghdad Pact. The Turkish and Iraqi governments had signed this mutual assistance pact, on February 24th 1955, for protection against threats from the Soviet Union. They were soon joined by Iran, Pakistan and Great Britain. Anthony Eden saw membership of the Pact as a sensible way of replacing the "unequal treaties", signed after World War I, which had allowed some British troops to be stationed in some Arab countries. Nasser was violently opposed to the Pact. He believed that it would prolong the existence of British influence in the Middle East.

The J.I.C. noted that, "the Baghdad Pact powers and Nuri in particular would be delighted to see Nasser brought down; but even in Iraq the press (apart from one government controlled paper) had welcomed Nasser's action ….. The Lebanese in general support Nasser's move. Nasser's action has won acclaim not only in Egypt but throughout the Middle East. King Hussein sent a congratulatory message (though he has tried to explain this away to our Ambassador); Thanksgiving sermons are reported to have been preached in the mosques of Damascus; in the Sudan, the step was welcomed by newspapers of all shades of opinion. King Saud has conveyed his unqualified support for

Egyptian action to Nasser ....."

The J.I.C. thought that Soviet economic aid to Egypt would offset any Western economic pressure on Nasser. "The Soviet government can be expected to pose as Egypt's and the Arab's best friend and to continue to give Egypt economic aid of all sorts; but they probably do not wish to risk a direct clash with the West in support of Colonel Nasser's ambitions and they may not wish to take on the whole burden of supporting Egypt financially and economically ..... The most satisfactory outcome from the Soviet point of view might be some sort of international discussions, preferably in the U.N., leading to an indecisive face-saving solution which would satisfy neither the West nor Egypt. The Soviet government would then have Colonel Nasser very much at its mercy and would be able to continue penetration of Egypt systematically and at leisure."

The J.I.C. predicted: "If only financial action is taken by the West, other Arab states might feel able to take steps to weaken their ties with, or dependence on, Great Britain, France and the United States. These steps might include (a) Jordan may call for drastic revision of the Anglo-Jordan Treaty. (b) Libya may denounce the Anglo-Libyan Treaty. (c) The Tunisian and Moroccan governments may adopt an even more intransigent attitude towards France (d) Syria and the Lebanon may stop or delay deliveries of oil from the Mediterranean terminals (e) Members of the Arab League may refuse transit, landing and refuelling facilities for British military aircraft. (f) Saudi Arabia may step up demands for a greater share of the profits from oil. (g) Our position may be weakened in Aden, Bahrain, Buraimi, Kuwait and Qatar. (h) Sabotage of oil installations might occur in any of the Arab states. (i) The effectiveness and cohesion of the Baghdad Pact might be undermined. (j) Nuri might feel we had not gone far enough towards bringing Nasser down and his own position in Iraq would become doubtful. (k) The position of the oil consortium in Iran would be greatly weakened."

After this unrelieved pessimism about the impact of nationalisation and its doubts about the effectiveness of economic pressure upon Colonel

Nasser, the J.I.C. was slightly less gloomy about the probable Arab reaction to armed intervention. "Although most, if not all, the Arab states would sympathise with Egypt, we do not think that in the event, they would come to her aid ..... We also doubt whether the Soviet Union would take any action ..... The Soviet government might send technicians and further arms to Egypt but we doubt whether, in the event of hostilities, these would greatly affect the issue ..... If steps taken by the West were to lead to an early change of government in Egypt ..... Iraq would expect to reap the benefits of her pro-Western attitude and to be set up in Egypt's place as the leader of the Arab world."

The J.I.C.'s pessimism returned when they noted, "should Western military action be insufficient to ensure early and decisive victory, the international consequences both in the Arab states and elsewhere might give rise to extreme embarrassment and cannot be forecast."

The J.I.C. finally discussed the impact of the Canal's nationalisation on the Arab-Israeli dispute. ".....We believe that Egypt is likely to tread warily ..... She would only make her position more difficult in the immediate future by aggression against Israel ..... On the other hand ..... whatever steps the West take, there will be a strong incentive to Israel to take military action against Egypt in the belief that the West will now no longer wish to prevent a blow at Nasser ..... Were Israel to attack Egypt while the West were merely applying some form of sanctions, the other Arab states would probably be forced by public opinion to go to Egypt's aid. If Israel attacked when Western forces were engaged with the Egyptians ..... the other Arab states would probably not join in, but great resentment would undoubtedly be created by what would be interpreted as a plot between Israel and the West."

The Entente Revived

The Joint Intelligence Committee's assessment of the situation in the Middle East had made only a passing reference to the French position; but, it was soon clear that the nationalisation of the Canal had given a new lease of life to the Anglo-French Entente Cordiale. On the day after nationalisation Admiral Henri Nomy, the French Chief of Naval staff, arrived in London to encourage a swift British military response. The French were even prepared to put their forces under British command. In a debate on August 1st in the French Chamber of Deputies, many of the speeches sounded even more belligerent than those in the House of Commons.

It was not surprising that the nationalisation of the Suez Canal Company had produced such a strong reaction in France. In the middle of the nineteenth century, French engineers, led by the redoubtable Ferdinand de Lesseps, had supervised the digging of the Canal which was opened in November 1869. Benjamin Disraeli, the British Prime Minister, had organised the purchase in 1875 of a substantial bloc of Suez Canal Company shares for the British government; but the Company's headquarters remained in Paris and the Company's ethos was French.

While the breaking of this historic connection provoked some irritation, the fierceness of the French reaction owed more to the belief that Nasser was supporting a violent rebellion in part of France - for in 1956 a clear majority of French parliamentarians believed that the three Algerian Departments of Algiers, Constantine and Oran were an integral part of France. In 1955, Tunisia and Morocco had become fully independent. But Algeria was different. There could be no retreat from Algeria.

The first rumbling of trouble in Algeria had taken place in the town of Setif on May 8th 1945 when a number of French civilians were killed in a wholly unexpected burst of violence. The main rebellion, however, did not break out until All Saint's Day 1954 when there were violent clashes in many parts of Algeria. There was a strong French military response. The bloodshed escalated sharply after the Philippeville massacre on August 20th 1955. According to official figures 71 Europeans were killed on August 20th while 1,273 "insurgents" died in the aftermath. Rebel leaders claimed that the true number of Muslims killed was as high as 12,000. A major conflict was now underway.

Apart from the communists, all the political parties in France supported the substantial military campaign now being waged in Algeria. As Pierre Mendès France, the French Prime Minister, who had led the French departure from Vietnam in 1954 said in the French Assembly: "one does not compromise when it comes to defending the internal peace of the nation, the unity and integrity of the Republic. The Algerian Departments are part of the French Republic ..... Between them and metropolitan France there can be no conceivable secession." By the beginning of 1955, the French Ministry of Defence and the French Intelligence Services were convinced that Nasser was playing a vital role in encouraging the Algerian revolt. The charismatic Jacques Soustelle, who had been the Minister in charge of Algerian Affairs at a pivotal moment, described Nasser as "the head of an octopus whose tentacles have, for so many months, been strangling French North Africa".

When Guy Mollet became Prime Minister after the election of January 2nd 1956, he increased the number of French troops in Algeria to 400,000. At first the new Foreign Minister, Christian Pineau, shared his officials' doubts about the importance of Nasser's support for the Algerian rebels. Shortly after meeting Nasser in Cairo, however, he also became convinced that the Egyptian leader was an implacable enemy. The most prominent leaders of the Algerian revolt were working in Cairo. A limited quantity of Egyptian weapons was being shipped to the rebels; but the most important, and most obvious, support for the rebellion came from Cairo Radio. Every day, in every village, Algerians could hear stirring messages on their wireless sets encouraging them to intensify the struggle.

The French difficulty in Algeria did not, however, attract much sympathy from her British and American allies. President Eisenhower, who had commanded the allied landings in French North Africa in 1942, dismissed as nonsense the idea that the Algerian Departments were actually part of metropolitan France. This negative view of Algerie Française was shared by large numbers of Britons who also believed passionately in the intrinsic Britishness of Gibraltar – a rock attached to the southern coast of Spain.

Israel, however, had already become a quietly enthusiastic French ally. As the Algerian revolt gathered momentum, Israeli military intelligence began to provide French military intelligence with considerable quantities of useful information about rebel activities and plans. This was received with particular gratitude by the substantial number of French Ministers who had fought in the Resistance during World War II and had a natural sympathy for the new Jewish State. In the autumn of 1955, after the Egyptian-Soviet arms deal had shattered the delicate arms balance in the Middle East, the British and American governments had refused to sell extra weapons to Israel. The French government, however, had offered guns as well as sympathy.

At the end of June 1956, on the eve of the nationalisation of the Suez Canal Company, the French Ministry of Defence was even considering joint operations with the Israelis against targets in Egypt - notably Cairo Radio. Some French Ministers saw the shock of nationalisation as an opportunity for encouraging Great Britain to join in a war against Nasser that they were already fighting. If President Nasser's government was going to be hit effectively, the French needed bases and bombers. The British could provide both.

Strains in a Special Relationship

Nasser's nationalisation of the Canal rang alarm bells in Washington. John Foster Dulles, the American Secretary of State was on a ceremonial visit to Peru; but Robert Murphy, the Assistant Secretary of State, was sent flying across the Atlantic to London. He had served as a diplomatic advisor to General Eisenhower in North Africa in 1943. There, he became a friend of Harold Macmillan who had been the British government's representative at the Eisenhower Headquarters.

On July 31st Murphy sent an urgent telegram to the Secretary of State for onward transmission to the President:

9

"..... I have had private, separate and lengthy talks with Eden and Macmillan ..... I want to segregate one urgent note both men struck which they requested be communicated in utter secrecy to you and the President. They said British Government has decided to drive Nasser out of Egypt. The decision they declared is firm. They expressed simple conviction. Military action is necessary and inevitable. In separate conversations each said in substance they ardently hoped U.S. would be with them in this determination, but if we could not they would understand and our friendship would be unimpaired. If we were with them from beginning chances of World War III would be far less than if we delayed. They seem convinced U.S.S.R. will not intervene but they assert that a risk must be taken. Macmillan repeated over and over in language similar to that employed by Eden that government had taken the decision and that Parliament and British people are with them."

"They both repeated the wish that the President clearly understand (that their) decision is firm and has been arrived at calmly and without emotion. They see no alternative. Macmillan in referring to our close wartime association in French North Africa emphasised several times his belief that as a former advisor and member of President's wartime staff he felt he could assure the President that Britain had no intention of submitting to Nasser's dictation, that British stake in M.E. is vital, that a demonstration of force provided only solution. Macmillan described some of the military planning which contemplates he said the landing of three British divisions in Egypt in an operation which would take six weeks to mount. The British estimate of importance of Egyptian resistance is low. Macmillan talked about costs. He said this operation would cost 4 to 5 hundred million pounds which they couldn't afford but they would pay. All British shipping would be allocated to it except the two Queens (the liners *Queen Mary* and *Queen Elizabeth*) ..... Eden, Macmillan and Lloyd showed throughout unexpected calm and no hysteria. They act as though they really have taken a decision after profound reflection. They are flexible on procedure leading up to a show down; but insist, over and over again, that whatever conferences, arrangements, public postures and manoeuvres might be necessary at the end they are determined to use force. They hope we will be with them and believe French are with them."

"At dinner Macmillan and Field Marshal Alexander (Harold Caccia only other person present) urged repeatedly that President as their former C. in C. (should) fully appreciate finality of British decision. Macmillan several times expressed wish he could explain all this orally to President. I apologise for length of this message but I am persuaded that flavour of their calm and very serious statements should be conveyed urgently as they request to the President."

In Washington, the American Chiefs of Staff were also talking about the use of force. In a memorandum for their Secretary of Defense they wrote: "the Joint Chiefs of Staff are seriously concerned with the implications of the recent Egyptian nationalisation of the Suez Maritime Canal Company. They consider this Egyptian action to be militarily detrimental to the United States and its Allies ..... The Joint Chiefs of Staff consider this Egyptian action with its attendant implications to be of such importance as to require action by the United States and its Allies which can reasonably be expected to result in placing the Suez Canal under a friendly and responsible authority at the earliest possible date. Furthermore, they believe that, if action short of the use of military force cannot reasonably be expected to achieve this result, the United States should consider the desirability of taking military action in support of the U.K., France and others as appropriate."

Within hours of receiving Robert Murphy's telegram from London – and before the American Joint Chiefs of Staff could deliver their own memorandum – the American President was sending an urgent letter to the British Prime Minister:

July 31, 1956

Dear Anthony,

From the moment that Nasser announced nationalisation of the Suez Canal Company, my thoughts have been constantly with you. Until this morning, I was happy to feel that we were approaching decisions as to applicable procedures somewhat along parallel lines, even though there were, as would be expected, important differences as to detail. But early this morning I received the messages, communicated to me through Murphy from you and Harold Macmillan, telling me on a most secret basis of your decision to employ force without delay or attempting any intermediate and less drastic steps.

We recognise the transcendent worth of the Canal to the free world and the possibility that eventually the use of force might become necessary in order to protect international rights. But we have been hopeful that through the Conference in which would be represented the signatories to the Convention of 1888, as well as other maritime nations, there would be brought about such pressures on the Egyptian government that the efficient operation of the Canal could be assured for the future.

For my part, I cannot over-emphasise the strength of my conviction that some such method must be attempted before action such as you contemplate should be undertaken. If unfortunately the situation can finally resolved only by drastic means, there should be no grounds for belief anywhere that corrective measures were undertaken merely to protect national or individual investors, or that the legal rights of a sovereign nation were ruthlessly flouted. A conference, at the very least, should have a great educational effect throughout the world. Public opinion here and, I am convinced in most of the world, would be outraged should there be a failure to make such efforts. Moreover, initial military successes might be easy, but the eventual price might become far too heavy.

I have given you my own personal conviction, as well as that of my associates, as to the un-wisdom even of contemplating the use of military force at this moment. Assuming, however, that the whole situation continued to deteriorate to the point where such action would seem the only recourse, there are certain political facts to remember.

As you realise, employment of United States forces is possible only through positive action on the part of the Congress, which is now adjourned but can be reconvened on my call for special reasons. If those reasons should involve the issue of employing United States military strength abroad there would have to be a showing that every peaceful means of resolving the difficulty had previously been exhausted. Without such a showing, there would be a reaction that could very seriously affect our peoples' feelings towards our Western Allies. I do not want to exaggerate, but I assure you that this could grow to such an intensity as to have the most far reaching consequences.

I realise that the messages from both you and Harold stressed that the decision taken was already approved by the government and was firm and irrevocable. But I personally feel that the American reaction would be severe and that great areas of the world would share that reaction. On the other hand, I believe we can marshal that opinion in support of a reasonable and conciliatory, but absolutely firm, position. So I hope that you will consent to reviewing this matter once more in its broadest aspects. It is for this reason that I have asked Foster to leave this afternoon to meet with your people in London.

I have given you here only a few highlights in the chain of reasoning that compels us to conclude that the step you contemplate should not be undertaken until every peaceful means of protecting the rights and livelihood of great portions of the world had been thoroughly explored and exhausted. Should these means fail, and I think it is erroneous to assume in advance that they needs must fail, then world opinion would understand how earnestly all of us had attempted to be just, fair and considerate, but that we simply could not accept a situation that would in the long run prove disastrous to the prosperity and living standards of every nation whose economy depends directly or indirectly upon East-West shipping.

With warm personal regard - and with earnest assurances of my continued respect and friendship,

With warm regard,

As ever,

D.E.

Within one week of the nationalisation of the Suez Canal Company, the Anglo-American special relationship was clearly going to be put under severe strain. The British Prime Minister and the American President were moving in opposite directions.

Preparing for a War

When the British Chiefs of Staff began to think about military intervention on the day after Nasser had nationalised the Suez Canal Company, it did not look as though they were faced with a particularly difficult task. On July 26th 1956 there were 750,000 men and women in the British Armed Forces which were the strongest in the Western world apart from the Americans. The senior British Commanders had all served with distinction in World War II.

General Sir Charles Keightley, who commanded British forces in the Middle East from his Headquarters in Cyprus, would soon be appointed as the overall Commander of any expeditionary force. He had been a Divisional Commander under General Eisenhower when the Allies landed in French North Africa in 1942. Lieutenant General, Sir Hugh Stockwell, who would command the land forces in any invasion of Egypt had commanded a Division in Burma at the end of World War II. In the five years from 1939 to 1944, Hugh Stockwell had risen from the rank of Major to Major General. In 1948 he had commanded 6th Airborne Division during the withdrawal from Palestine. Almost every battalion in the British Army contained some men who had fought in World War II.

The pro-Greek EOKA terrorist campaign on Cyprus, which had begun in April 1955, fortuitously meant that the British garrison on the island had expanded. 16 Parachute Brigade had already spent some months chasing EOKA terrorists. They were joined in the Cypriot mountains by 3 Commando Brigade as well as six ordinary infantry battalions.

The British planners also had to face the fact that British bases in the area were inadequate. Cyprus was 300 miles from Port Said and Malta was 1000 miles. Cyprus had the ports and airfields closest to Egypt (once it had been decided that the use of Libya was politically out of bounds). There were three cramped airfields on the island and only one of them was fully operational in July 1956. There was only one Cypriot port, Famagusta, where tanks could actually be loaded onto landing craft; but there were no tanks on the island and no landing craft to carry them.

In June 1944, 800 L.C.T.s (Tank Landing Craft) had provided the backbone of the D–Day invasion fleet. In July 1956 there were only two L.C.T.s and two of the larger L.S.T.s (Landing Ship Tank) stationed in the Mediterranean as part of the Amphibious Warfare Squadron in Malta. Air mobility was provided by elderly Dakota, Hastings and Valetta aircraft; and there were only enough of them to carry one battalion of the Parachute Regiment into battle. This reflected the low priority given to mobility in post–Word War II defence procurement programs.

After a British force had landed on Egyptian soil, it would be faced by an Egyptian army of 100,000 men, half of whom were stationed in Sinai or the Canal Zone. The regular army, which consisted of one armoured division and three infantry divisions, was backed by a freshly recruited National Guard and a semi–militarised police force. There was no doubt that the Egyptian Armed Forces would be well-equipped. The Czech-Egyptian arms deal which had been made public in September 1955 meant that the Egyptian Army was receiving: 300 tanks, 100 armoured self-propelled guns as well as substantial supplies of armoured personnel carriers and artillery. The Egyptian Airforce would be equipped with over 100 MIG 15 fighters and IL28 bombers.

But would the Egyptian Army fight; and would they be able to use their new weapons? Within the British defence establishment opinion was sharply divided. In their first post-nationalisation report, the Joint Intelligence Committee had said ..... "Egypt is unlikely to be proficient in ..... (the use of her new weapons) ..... before the end of 1956. Although the morale of the

15

Egyptian Armed Forces is at present likely to be high we consider that the temperament of the Egyptian people is such that were they themselves subject to immediate physical danger their morale would probably collapse; and the downfall of Nasser might result".

In an appendix to their report, however, the J.I.C. gave a quite different assessment of the Egyptian Army's capability. They looked back to 1948 when the Egyptian Army had advanced towards Tel Aviv in an attempt to crush the new state of Israel; but, after some initial success, the amateur soldiers of Israel had routed the Egyptians. Major Nasser had served in one of the units covering the Egyptian retreat. As the J.I.C. explained, "the failure of the Egyptian Army against the Israelis in 1948 was largely due, not to the lack of fighting ability of the Egyptian troops, but to the inadequacy of the higher command. The fat, dissolute senior commanders of the Farouk era have now been replaced by younger professional soldiers, who, while lacking in experience, cannot but be better than their predecessors ..... Although it has been customary to decry the efficiency of the Egyptian soldier in the past, we feel that ..... it would be dangerous at this time to underestimate the capability of the Army, which, although untested under fire since 1948, has developed and improved during the past few years."

The J.I.C.'s schizophrenia also infected the Ministry of Defence. When news of the nationalisation had reached 10 Downing Street, the First Sea Lord, Admiral Lord Louis Mountbatten, had talked about a lightning strike at Port Said. The Mediterranean Fleet, which was assembled at Malta, could pick up part of 3 Commando Brigade in Cyprus and seize Port Said within a week. By August 3rd, however, all thoughts of a lightning assault had been abandoned. Some of the army planners remembered the police station action in Ismailia in January 1952 when a force of 100 Egyptian policemen had ignored an order to surrender to a substantial British force and had resisted with unexpected courage. Lieutenant-General Sir Hugh Stockwell now began the instructions to his planners with the words, "we can neither afford to lose nor risk a setback". There were few prizes to be won by mounting a bold assault on Egypt, while there clearly would be sharp criticism for any commander whose troops lost the smallest skirmish.

By the middle of August the planners for the operation, which was given the code name *Musketeer*, were thinking of a deployment of 50,000 men from Great Britain supported by 100 Royal Navy warships including five aircraft carriers carrying a total of 150 aircraft. Altogether 12,000 vehicles and 300 aircraft would be involved. The recall of the Reserves, which had been announced by the Prime Minister in the House of Commons on August 2nd, would affect 25,000 men. Two weeks after nationalisation, the Ministry of Defence was beginning to assemble the forces needed for the largest British military operation since the end of World War II. It could not be launched before September 15th.

This presented considerable logistical problems. Some of the tanks, which were going to be loaded on ships at Portsmouth, had to be transported across Salisbury Plain by Pickford's, the leading furniture removal firm. A force of this size could not be kept at a high state of readiness for long without causing unusual strain within the armed forces; but, if any significant part of this force were to be sent home, it would be interpreted as a sign that the government was relaxing its pressure on Egypt. The decision to recall a substantial number of reservists now added to the political pressure for swift action. If the reservists were to be kept in uniform for many weeks, there were bound to be vigorous complaints from their families.

An Armed Entente

There was also going to be a massive contribution from the French. They would provide 30,000 men alongside the British contribution of 50,000. There would be 30 French warships including two French aircraft carriers and a French battleship. In their enthusiasm to speed operations against the Egyptians, the French readily agreed that there would be a British Commander in Chief with a French Deputy. The Commanders of the Air, Land, & Naval Forces would also be British with French Deputies. The French would provide 9,000 vehicles and 200 aircraft.

The French had different weapons which were sometimes more modern than those carried by British soldiers. Some of the ammunition was different. The rations were different, with a daily dose of red wine for the French. And the language was different. When a French advance guard arrived in Cyprus, their drivers were greeted with signs saying "Tennez à la Gauche". The French drivers adapted reasonably quickly to the problem of driving on the left hand side of the road: but, the problem of providing bilingual air support was more difficult. Some of the French pilots spoke English; very few of the British pilots spoke French. Should French signallers be attached to British units?

The first attempts to co-ordinate this allied effort did not run entirely smoothly. When a French contingent of senior officers led by General Beaufré, the Deputy Land Force Commander, arrived in London on August 10th they were shown into a meeting that was being briefed by Lieutenant General Sir Hugh Stockwell. Minutes before the arrival of the French, General Stockwell had received a message telling him that the operational plans should not be revealed to the French "for security reasons". General Stockwell's Chief of Staff noted with admiration that the General proceeded to describe an entirely fictitious plan in front of his combined audience.

This was the first of many unfortunate incidents. The French planners who came to London did not like their small underground offices, nor did the French like being presented with a British plan and then asked to comment. This was not their idea of joint planning.

A Secret Alliance

Five days before the nationalisation of the Canal Company, General Moshe Dayan, the Chief of Staff of the Israeli Defence Forces, flew to Vermars, a small town 15 kilometres south of Paris, for a meeting with leading members of the French defence establishment. As the head of the French Military Intelligence said in his opening remarks, they had come together to examine ways to "thwart Nasser's initiatives". Dayan responded by saying, "the Arab empire Nasser is dreaming about will not arise unless Israel surrenders ....."

As soon as the details of the Czech-Egyptian arms deal had become clear after September 1955, the Israeli government was sure that Nasser was preparing to attack them in the near future. Egypt did not need scores of jet bombers or hundreds of heavily armoured tanks for use against her other neighbours - Libya or the Sudan. Nasser's hostile intentions were confirmed by his imposition of a blockade of the Straits of Tiran. This cut Israeli access to Asia and Africa. It was the quality as well as the quantity of weapons involved that had alarmed the Israelis. As Dayan had written, "a brilliant pilot in a propeller aircraft has no chance against a mediocrity in a jet. A daring tank gunner in an obsolete Sherman, which is the tank we had, would find his shells bouncing off the armour of a Stalin-3 tank, which was what the Egyptians were about to receive".

In 1954, Egypt had also backed an intensification of cross-border terrorist attacks. In the five years, 1951 to 1955, an average of three Israelis a week – out of a Jewish population of less that two million – had been killed by Arab marauders. Not all these attacks were politically motivated: but, in the eighteen months before the nationalisation of the Canal, Egyptian Intelligence Officers had sponsored and directed an increasing number of raids from Jordan and from Gaza. In 1955, more than 200 Israelis had been killed in Fedayeen attacks.

There were also the numerous anti-Israeli passages in Nasser's book, *The Philosophy of the Revolution*. Not only had Nasser written at length about his schoolboy demonstrations in the 1930s against Zionist immigration to Palestine; but Nasser had also described in great detail his visits in 1948 to the elderly Mufti of Jerusalem, who had orchestrated the Palestinian Arab rebellion of 1936, and who was now living in Egypt. Nasser claimed that in early 1948 he had offered to recruit a group of Egyptian Officers to fight in Palestine. The Israeli Prime Minister, David Ben-Gurion, who had originally welcomed Nasser's rise to power, had read Nasser's book and had been convinced of Nasser's hostility.

At the Vermars Conference, where there had been some discussion of Franco-Israeli joint operations inside Egypt, the main result had been a secret agreement for the transfer of very substantial quantities of French equipment to the Israelis. Apart from jet aircraft, Dayan wanted, and got, substantial numbers of four-wheel drive trucks. As he pointed out, "our big problem was vehicles fit for movement in the desert. I did not know how tough the opposition from Egyptian armour would be, but I did know how serious an obstacle the desert was".

After Nationalisation Day, the French were ready to expand their operational partnership with Israel. The British, however, were anxious not to get involved with the Israelis. Two days after nationalisation, the British Ambassador to Israel delivered a warning note to the Israeli government telling them that they should not make any move against Nasser.

There was, however, one British Cabinet Minister who wanted to use the Israelis "to make faces" at the Egyptians. Harold Macmillan did not share the general view of the Foreign Office that an Israeli thrust into Sinai would consolidate Arab support for Nasser. The Israelis had a valid legal excuse for acting. The blockade of the Straits of Tiran was plainly illegal. If the Israeli army could now quickly defeat the Egyptian forces in Sinai, Nasser's prestige would suffer a mortal blow. An Israeli advance into Sinai would also protect the flanks of an Anglo-French operation in the Canal zone. Harold Macmillan knew that the Israeli government had openly discussed the possibility of moving into Sinai to break the Egyptian blockade. Meanwhile, any fighting in Sinai would give the British and the French a valid excuse for re-occupying the Canal zone. Eden, however, vetoed Macmillan's suggestion and would not let it be discussed by the Egypt Committee.

Personal Bitterness

On August 8th Anthony Eden made a Prime Ministerial broadcast about the Canal Company's nationalisation. He restated many of the points that he had made in the debate in the House of Commons on August 2nd. The oil shipped through the Canal was vital for the whole of Western Europe, "without it, machinery and much of our transport would grind to a halt". Colonel Nasser "has taken over an international company without consultation and without consent".

There was a sharper note in the Prime Minister's voice, however, when he went on to criticise Colonel Nasser's conduct. "Our quarrel is not with Egypt, still less with the Arab world; it is with Colonel Nasser. When he gained power in Egypt we felt no hostility towards him. On the contrary, we made agreements with him. We hoped that he wanted to improve the conditions of life for his people and to be friends with this country. He told us that he wanted a new spirit in Anglo-Egyptian relations. We welcomed that. But instead of meeting us with friendship, Colonel Nasser conducted a vicious propaganda campaign against this country. He has shown that he is not a man who can be trusted to keep an agreement ..... The pattern is familiar to many of us ..... We all know this is how fascist governments behave, and we all remember, only to well, what the cost can be of giving in to fascism."

Anthony Eden's two principal political lieutenants had markedly different reactions to the Prime Minister's bellicose broadcast. Harold Macmillan, who was now Chancellor of the Exchequer – after a brief spell as Foreign Secretary - noted in his diary, "this could not have been better done. It was fair, moderate, convincing and firm. I'm sure it will have a splendid effect at home and abroad." It did not, however, have a splendid effect on R.A. Butler, the Leader of the House of Commons, who recorded his depression on hearing the Prime Minister's broadcast. "My mood was of deep misgiving and anxiety on hearing this analogy with fascism and this personalisation of Nasser."

It was hardly surprising, however, that the Prime Minister should feel personally embittered by Nasser's action. For almost two years after Colonel Nasser had emerged as the leader of the Egyptian government in 1954, Anthony Eden had been ready to defend Colonel Nasser's behaviour, even if this provoked friction on his own back-benches.

These anxieties had been stirred by Eden's handling of an issue on which he had unrivalled expertise. As a young Foreign Secretary, he had been personally involved in the negotiation of the Anglo-Egyptian Treaty of 1936 which provided the legal basis for the British presence in the Canal zone. In recognition of his skill in drafting the treaty, Eden's face had subsequently appeared on a series of Egyptian stamps.

In 1940, when Nasser was stationed in Khartoum as a young Lieutenant in the Egyptian Army, Eden had been the Cabinet Minister responsible for seeing that General Wavell had the resources he needed to defeat the Italian Army in Libya. Lieutenant Nasser felt personally humiliated when the British Ambassador ordered King Farouk to change his Prime Minister on February 4th 1942, after British troops had surrounded the Royal Palace. As Foreign Secretary, Anthony Eden had approved of this unusual exercise of British authority.

When he returned to the Foreign Office after the Conservative victory at the General Election of 1951, Eden clearly recognised the over-riding importance of reaching a satisfactory agreement with the Egyptians on the future of the enormous Canal base which sprawled over an area the size of Wales. In 1951, it was guarded by 80,000 British soldiers.

There were difficulties on every side. In Egypt, in 1952, a series of weak Egyptian Prime Ministers under King Farouk tried to enhance their popularity by encouraging anti-British campaigns. There were strikes and attacks on British soldiers in the Canal zone. There were murderous riots in Cairo. In July, 1952, King Farouk was forced to abdicate after a military coup.

In 1953, negotiations with the young officers who ran the new Egyptian government moved slowly. The Prime Minister, Winston Churchill was incapacitated by a serious stroke and Anthony Eden's health was damaged by a faulty bile-duct operation. In Cairo there was some uncertainty about whether General Neguib or Colonel Nasser was the dominant force in the Revolutionary Council.

In Washington, the Republican Administration was taking over from President Truman's Democrats after President Eisenhower's inauguration in January 1953. John Foster Dulles had become the Secretary of State. Dulles and Eden had occasionally met during the previous decade. They had rarely agreed. According to Dulles's principal biographer, Anthony Eden tried to persuade Eisenhower privately not to appoint Dulles as Secretary of State. In the spring of 1953, the new Secretary of State made his first visit to the Middle East. He was impressed by the strength of Arab nationalism. In a memorandum which he wrote on his return Dulles noted that, "almost the entire area is caught in a fanatical revolutionary spirit." He also argued that the British and French influence in the area was collapsing and that the 'Israeli factor' plus the Arab tendency to link the United States with the colonial policies of European states were "millstones around our neck". President Eisenhower seemed to agree with the Dulles argument that if America did not help the new generation of Arab nationalists there was a danger that the Soviet Union would win the battle for hearts and minds in the Middle East. In Cairo, the American Central Intelligence Agency had decided that Colonel Nasser would soon emerge as the dominant force in the Revolutionary Council. Nasser liked Americans – he was addicted to Hollywood movies – and the C.I.A. liked him.

By the middle of 1954, many of these issues had been resolved. After a tense internal struggle, Colonel Nasser had emerged as the dominant figure in Egypt. At Westminster, Winston Churchill had regained much of his strength and retained his doubts about the need to withdraw from Suez. At the Foreign Office, Eden was engaged in a remarkable year of diplomatic negotiation, which would have taxed the strength of a man with a platinum bile-duct. The long-standing dispute between Italy and Yugoslavia over Trieste was settled on Eden's initiative. When the French Assembly defeated attempts to facilitate German re-armament by voting against the proposal for a European Defence

Community, Eden, once again, played a major role in resolving this problem through the establishment of a Western European Union. In the Far East, Eden had restrained Dulles's enthusiasm for a strong military intervention to support the crumbling French position in Indochina. There was widespread approval when Eden's remarkable year of diplomatic achievement was marked by his installation as a Knight of the Garter.

There was less widespread applause for Eden's willingness to reach agreement with Colonel Nasser's Egyptian government about a partial withdrawal from the Canal base and the departure of all British troops from the banks of the Canal. A sizeable number of Conservative Members of Parliament were opposed to the idea of a complete withdrawal. These doubts were shared by the Prime Minister, Winston Churchill, who, as a young Subaltern had taken part in the Battle of Omdurman which, in 1898, secured the Sudan for British administration.

Despite the Prime Minister's mutterings about 'Munich on the Nile' Anthony Eden saw little point in postponing a decision. The withdrawal of British troops from Egypt was clearly one of Nasser's main objectives, while British doubts about the military value of the base had increased substantially after the successful testing of a hydrogen bomb.

On July 28th 1954, Anthony Eden announced in the House of Commons the result of the negotiations. British troops would be withdrawn 20 months after the signing of a formal agreement. The equipment left in the base would be looked after by civilians hired by British firms. The base would be reactivated and used by British troops if there was an attack on any member of the Arab League or on Turkey.

After Anthony Eden had made his statement, Clement Attlee, who was still Leader of the Opposition, asked, "in view of the statements which were made by the present Prime Minister (Winston Churchill) on the absolute necessity of having troops in Egypt for the defence of the Suez Canal; and the violent language which he used when any proposal was put forward from this side of the House for withdrawal from Egypt, may I ask whether this agreement has the Prime Minister's consent?" Unusually, Winston Churchill, who was sitting next to his Foreign Secretary, then rose and told the House, "I am convinced that it is absolutely necessary".

In a short debate on the following day Julian Amery, a leader of the Suez sceptics and a son-in-law of Harold Macmillan, launched a savage attack on the agreement. "It is the end of a process which has lasted seventy-two years. It is seventy-two years since we went into Egypt at the behest ..... of a liberal administration under Mr. Gladstone. Seventy-two years which Colonel Nasser described yesterday as 'seventy-two years of bitterness' ..... It is an area in which the forces of the Commonwealth came twice in a generation to defend freedom and civilisation. There has been a very difficult position in the area in the last three years. There has been a state of siege. Now, the garrison is to march out with the full honours of war, but after submitting to a full capitulation."

In answering the critics among his own supporters, Anthony Eden argued, "it is ludicrous to pretend that as a result of this agreement our influence is going to be undermined throughout the Middle East ..... The conditions as they exist now in all these countries, their sentiments, their national feelings, bear no parallel to those of even fifteen, let alone twenty, years ago ..... Through this agreement with Egypt we shall be creating a new pattern of friendship ..... It is the only way we can hope to work with these countries. We cannot hope to work with them by putting 20,000, 30,000, 80,000 men there and telling them what to do ..... I want us in this House to say plainly to Egypt tonight that we are going to enter into this new era with a real determination to try and make it succeed".

Eden's call for the creation of "a new pattern of friendship" in the Middle East carried the day. 257 Members - almost all Conservative - supported the agreement. The Parliamentary Labour Party officially abstained. Only 26 sceptics went into the 'No' lobby with Julian Amery.

Nasser's Ambitions

The final negotiation of the Anglo-Egyptian Canal Base Agreement now moved forward smoothly. When it was signed in Cairo at the end of October, there was much talk by the Egyptian delegation about N.E.C.M.U. - the New Era of Co-operation and Mutual Understanding. There was a promise that the daily dose of anti-British propaganda which poured out of Cairo Radio would now stop. Perhaps there really would be a new era of co-operation. As Anthony Eden was to write nearly fifteen years later in his memoirs, the Egyptians then "showed no signs as yet of those wider ambitions of Empire which Colonel Nasser was later to proclaim and pursue. On balance, the agreement seemed to be to our advantage and worth a trial."

A few months before the new agreement had been signed, however, Colonel Nasser had produced some important evidence about his "wider ambitions of Empire". In the summer of 1954, Colonel Nasser's book, *The Philosophy of the Revolution*, was published. On September 14th 1954, Sir Ralph Stevenson, the British Ambassador in Cairo, had sent Anthony Eden a note about the book - a note which must rank as one of the more curious book reviews written by a British Ambassador in the 20th century. "The book throws a not unfavourable light upon its writer's own beliefs ..... His book has a certain breadth of vision, humanity and idealism which one might be excused for not expecting from a man of his background. It is encouraging to be able to record that this idealism and moral conviction appears to be standing the test of time."

While Sir Ralph was detecting "a certain breadth of vision, humanity and idealism" in Colonel Nasser's book, Part 3 of *The Philosophy of the Revolution* contained a searing denunciation of British imperialism. While the book's literary style owed much to Mohamed Heikel, a journalist who was Nasser's favourite spokesman, the ideas were clearly those of Nasser himself. According to Nasser, many of Egypt's political problems were the fault of British imperialism. "Even Israel itself is but a result of imperialism; for if Palestine had not fallen under the British mandate, Zionism would never have been able to muster enough support to realise a national home in Palestine. The idea would have remained a mad, hopeless dream ..... Imperialism is the great force that is imposing a murderous invisible siege upon the whole region."

Nasser believed, however, that imperialism could be beaten. "I do not doubt for a moment that our common effort will achieve for us ..... everything we desire. For I shall always maintain that we are strong. The only trouble is that we do not realise just how strong we are."

Nasser argued that there were three main sources of Arab strength. "The first of these sources is that we are a community of neighbouring peoples linked by all the material and moral ties possible, and that we have characteristics and abilities and a civilisation which has given rise to three holy religions ....."

"As for the second source of strength, it is our land itself, and its position on the map - that important strategic position which embraces the cross-roads of the world, the thoroughfare of its traders and the passageway of its armies".

"There remains the third source: oil - the sinew of material civilisation without which all its machines would cease to function. The great factories ..... all the instruments of land, air and sea communication; all the weapons of war from the mechanical bird above the clouds to the submarine beneath the waves - without oil all would turn back to naked metal, covered with rust, incapable of motion or use."

Nasser went on to quote extensively from an article published by the University of Chicago about world oil production. "The cost of producing a barrel of oil in North America is 78 cents. In South America 48 cents. But in Arab counties the cost is only 10 cents ..... It is a fact too, that average daily production per well is 11 barrels in the United States, 230 barrels in Venezuela and 4000 barrels in the Arab area. Have I made clear how great is the importance of this element of strength? I hope so. So we are strong - strong not in the loudness of our voices when we wail or shout for help but rather when we remain silent and measure the extent of our ability to act." Nasser was clearly thinking about the oil weapon.

Project Alpha

Following a long discussion between Nasser and Anthony Nutting, the Foreign Office Minister of State, after the signing of the Canal base agreement, Anthony Eden had come to the conclusion that Nasser would be the Arab leader most likely to reach a real peace agreement with Israel. In the first months of 1955 officials from the British Foreign Office and the American State Department spent much time trying to devise a scheme - codenamed *Alpha* - which would reduce Egyptian-Israeli tension. It was known that Nasser wanted a land-link with the Arabs in the East. This was blocked by Israel's occupation of the Negev, a wedge of desert that ran from the Israeli town of Beersheba, south of Tel Aviv to the embryonic Israeli port of Eilat on the Gulf of Aquaba. The negotiations did not go smoothly. Nasser wanted the whole of the Negev while Ben-Gurion and most Israeli Ministers did not wish to part with a single sand dune.

In the summer of 1955 Anthony Eden's enthusiasm for working with Nasser was put under new strain. Cairo Radio's attacks on "British Imperialism" were replaced by denunciations of the Baghdad Pact as a front for imperialism. There were also worrying reports that Nasser was about to sign a massive contract for the purchase of modern weapons from the Soviet Union, although the weapons would nominally come from Czecholovakia. For the last five years, Great Britain, France and the United States had tried to limit the flow of weapons to countries in the Middle East. On May 25th 1950, Great Britain, France and the United States had launched the Tripartite Declaration which said that the three powers would intervene against any Middle Eastern country which tried to breach the 1949 frontiers or armistice lines. The Tripartite agreement was also meant to keep a balance in the sale of weapons to Israel and her Arab neighbours. As Great Britain, France and America were the principal manufacturers of weapons in the West, this Tripartite control of arms sales had been remarkably effective. Now the Czech Arms Deal would clearly destroy this balance.

The news that Nasser was going to buy modern weapons from a

Communist country caused consternation in Washington and Whitehall. The American Minister responsible for the Middle East was dispatched from the State Department to Cairo in order to threaten the end of American aid for Egypt. The CIA continued to believe that Nasser was a friend, who could be saved from the embrace of the Soviet Union; but Dulles was more pessimistic. When Harold Macmillan dined with Dulles, days after the announcement of the contract, the Secretary of State asked Macmillan whether the British could halt their withdrawal from the Canal Zone. Macmillan did not think that this was possible.

Farewell to Glubb

Anthony Eden was still prepared to give Nasser the benefit of the doubt. The Middle East department of the Foreign office was inclined to believe Nasser's argument that he had been forced to seek weapons from the Communist bloc because of an Israeli raid near Gaza. In February 1955, an Israeli Commando Unit commanded by Colonel Ariel Sharon had launched a reprisal raid against an Egyptian headquarters in the Gaza strip. After unexpectedly fierce fighting, Sharon's men had inflicted the heaviest defeat on an Egyptian Army unit since the 1949 Armistice Agreement.

In the aftermath of the arms deal, Eden had supported and encouraged the American government's decision not to make extra arms available to Israel. Eden had also argued that extra Western aid should be made available to Egypt for the construction of the Aswan Dam. He also hoped that the arrival of the Czech weapons in Egypt would persuade the Israeli government to withdraw from part of the Negev. Six weeks after the announcement of the signing of the arms contract, Eden called for Israeli territorial concessions in a major speech at the Guildhall. The Egyptian press was mildly complimentary about Eden's speech. Israeli Ministers were outraged.

Eden's conciliatory policy had not, however, earned any respite from

Cairo Radio's violent assault on the members of the Baghdad Pact. The Iraqi and Jordanian governments were particular targets. This verbal attack was intensified when General Templer, the C.I.G.S., visited Jordan in December 1955 on a mission to try and persuade the Jordanian government to join the Baghdad Pact. Templer's visit was not a success; and then, on March 1st 1956, Glubb Pasha was dismissed from his post as Commander of the Arab Legion – Jordan's Army.

In British eyes, Glubb Pasha was the symbolic heir of Lawrence of Arabia, the young British officer who had promoted and guided the Arab Revolt in World War I. After serving with the Royal Engineers in France in World War I, John Bagot Glubb had moved to Mesopotamia where he had shown exceptional talent in leading and disciplining Bedouin tribesmen in a long-running campaign against Wahabi raiders from Saudi Arabia. Glubb was so successful that in 1939 he was appointed by King Abdullah of Jordan to command the Arab Legion. During World War II he had led the Arab Legion in successful attacks on pro-Nazi forces in Iraq. In 1948, Glubb's Arab Legion had been the most successful of the five Arab armies that had invaded Israel after the new Jewish state had proclaimed its independence. Now he was given less than 24 hours notice to leave Jordan with his family which included his adopted Palestinian children.

Even before Nasser's propaganda campaign there had been some Jordanian criticism of the fact that a British soldier should be commanding the Jordanian army. King Hussein's sudden dismissal of Glubb Pasha may well have been triggered by reading an article about Glubb in Country Life which was entitled. "The Uncrowned King of Jordan". Selwyn Lloyd, who had become Foreign Secretary after Harold Macmillan moved to the Treasury, was in Cairo when Glubb Pasha was dismissed. He was convinced that Nasser had engineered Glubb Pasha's departure. Selwyn Lloyd's mood was not improved when he was met in Bahrain by a stone-throwing crowd shouting pro-Nasser slogans.

On March 7th, Anthony Eden replied to an emergency debate in the

House of Commons on the Jordanian situation. It was one of the worst speeches that he had delivered in his long parliamentary career. At one point he lost his temper and shouted, "Really, the House must listen to the Prime Minister". As his wife, Clarissa, noted in her diary, "tonight's winding-up of the debate was a shambles". Five days later, Evelyn Shuckburgh, the head of the Foreign Office's Middle East department noted Eden's sharp comment about the need to remove Nasser, "its either him or us, don't forget that".

It was hardly surprising that Eden should feel that he had been personally let down by the Egyptian leader. Since he came to power in 1954, Nasser had made no secret of his wish to diminish British interests in the whole Middle East. Now the nationalisation of the Suez Canal Company made Eden's repeated attempts to excuse Nasser's conduct look a bit ridiculous. Eden did not like being made to look a bit ridiculous. For Eden, Nasser's plotting had been a stab in the front.

Lurching to the Left

While Anthony Eden was sharpening the tone of his criticism of Nasser, Hugh Gaitskell was under pressure within his own party to withdraw the verbal support that he had given to the Prime Minister during the debate on August 2nd.

A substantial cross-section of the Parliamentary Labour Party did not approve of their leader's criticism of President Nasser. Anthony Wedgewood Benn, the radical young Member of Parliament for Bristol South East, played a prominent role in organising the Suez Emergency Committee which would try to mobilise public opinion against the use of force. They could count on the support of Party militants all over the country. The hard left/crypto-communists in the Parliamentary Labour Party had supported President Nasser from the moment that he had signed the Czech-Egyptian arms contract. The more fervent anti-imperialists believed that the nationalisation of the canal was a victory for the oppressed masses in the third world.

While Gaitskell could expect criticism from the left, he also found that some of his right-wing allies in the Labour Party's recent policy disputes were pressing for a change of tone. Douglas Jay had been a friend of Hugh Gaitskell's since they had been schoolboys at Winchester College. Now, Douglas Jay argued that there should be no use of force without the specific approval of the United Nations. In this he was joined by Denis Healey, who had recently become a Member of Parliament after running the Labour Party's International Department for seven years. With the passive encouragement of Hugh Gaitskell, Douglas Jay and Denis Healey wrote a letter to the Times on August 7th attacking that newspaper's bellicose editorials and decrying the use of force without the specific authority of the United Nations. (The only part of Hugh Gaitskell's August 2nd speech that many senior Members of the Parliamentary Labour Party wished to remember was the brief peroration about the sanctity of the United Nations Charter.)

In the ideological civil war which had convulsed the Labour Party since its defeat in the 1951 General Election, Hugh Gaitskell had often clashed violently with Aneurin Bevan, the leading orator of the Party's left wing. Now, ironically, Nye Bevan defended the bellicose tone of Gaitskell's speech during some of Labour Party's post-debate inquests. Bevan thought that Nasser was a thug and he was later quoted as saying, "the only slogan sillier than 'My Country right or wrong' is the 'United Nations right or wrong'" but now reference to the United Nations was the only policy supported by all sections of the Party.

Meanwhile, after Hugh Gaitskell had gone on holiday to Pembrokeshire, there had been a friendly exchange of letters with the Prime Minister. On August 9th, Anthony Eden sent a chatty note about arrangements for the Suez Canal Users Conference which was being organised by the British Government and was due to meet in London on August 16th. The government hoped that the Conference - to which all the major users of the Canal had been invited - would endorse a scheme for the international management of the Canal. ".....

The acceptances to the Conference are coming in well. The response has been steadier and better than I expected ..... As far as Nehru was concerned the British High Commissioner ..... has the impression that he is moving towards the acceptance of some form at least of internationalisation. We shall see."

In his response, Hugh Gaitskell made it clear that he was not, in fact, in sympathy with the Prime Minister's policy. "..... Lest there should still be any doubt in your mind about my personal attitude, let me say that I could not regard an armed attack on Egypt by ourselves and the French as justified by anything which Nasser has done so far ..... If, of course, the whole matter were to be taken to the United Nations and if Egypt were to be condemned by them as aggressors, then, of course, the position would be different."

On August 14th, Hugh Gaitskell and two Shadow Cabinet colleagues saw Eden with Lord Salisbury and Selwyn Lloyd at 10 Downing Street. As Hugh Gaitskell noted in his diary, "we had a good forty minutes discussion with them urging our points ..... and in particular the desirability of their making a statement that the precautionary military measures were purely for self-defence. We did not get very far with them; they were very cautious in their replies and rather evasive." Eden, on the other hand, had been depressed by Gaitskell's "tedious lecture". The hope that the Prime Minister and the Leader of the Opposition could happily cooperate in trying to resolve the Canal crisis was now disappearing rapidly.

The Users Unite

While Eden's meeting with Gaitskell had been a disappointment, the performance of John Foster Dulles at the User's Conference exceeded British expectations. Dulles noted that international confidence ..... "had been grievously assaulted" by the nationalisation. With strong guidance from Dulles, the Conference passed a resolution calling for the establishment of a Suez Canal Board which should have the necessary authority to operate, maintain, develop and enlarge the Suez Canal. The operation of the Canal would be "insulated" from the politics of any nation. Egypt would get a generous share of the Canal revenue. Eden was pleased when 18 of the 22 countries at the conference signed the resolution that Dulles had advocated so strongly. Only the Soviet Union, India, Indonesia and Ceylon refused to sign. Eden had hoped that Dulles would lead a five nation delegation - Australia, Ethiopia, Iran, Sweden and the United States - which would present the Conference resolution to President Nasser. In fact, the task went to Robert Menzies, the Australian Prime Minister.

On August 24th, while the Menzies delegation was on its way to Cairo, Hugh Gaitskell saw the American Secretary of State at the American Embassy. According to the American Embassy memorandum of their conversation, "Gaitskell said that in his opinion 'H.M.G. could not successfully go it alone in the use of force' and the Labour Party would be strongly opposed to any armed action which could not be brought within the U.N. Mr. Gaitskell thought that not only would the Labour Party be strongly opposed, but at least half the nation. Mr. Dulles then urged Mr. Gaitskell to remember the national interest. The Secretary (Dulles) remarked that in times of crisis like the present one it was absolutely essential for a nation to give the appearance of unity; that any appearance of weakness or division was always taken advantage of by the enemy."

As Dulles was to report to President Eisenhower: "the attitude of the Labour Party is a hard blow for the government at this juncture, when bi-partisan unity would give Britain the best chance of retrieving its position without actually having to use force. I have no doubt that Nasser is fully aware of the situation and may calculate that, if he stands firm, the result will not be solid strength against him but perhaps a Labour government which would be softer."

Legal Doubts

On August 24th, while the Leader of the Opposition was talking to the American Secretary of State, Walter Monckton startled his fellow members of the Cabinet's Egypt Committee by a vigorous display of his political and legal doubts about *Musketeer*, the code name for the planned invasion. As the Defence Minister, Walter Monckton was nominally in charge of producing the plans which he was now criticising. After Walter Monckton's powerful critique, three members of the Egypt Committee wrote letters of encouragement to the Prime Minister; but, as Alan Lennox-Boyd, the Colonial Secretary, noted: "If there really is uncertainty in the Cabinet, we can't be surprised if it exists in the Country."

Within the Ministry of Defence, Walter Monckton's doubts about the wisdom of embarking upon *Musketeer* were encouraged by the First Sea Lord, Admiral Mountbatten. In the discussion after dinner, when news of Nasser's nationalisation reached 10 Downing Street, the Admiral had talked of a swift strike at Port Said. By the end of the following week, however, the First Sea Lord was putting his political doubts on paper. He wrote a number of letters questioning the wisdom of launching *Musketeer*. Some of these letters were shown to Ministers in the Ministry of Defence.

In the first discussions after nationalisation, the robust views of Lord Kilmuir, the Lord Chancellor, carried the day when he argued that Great Britain had a strong legal case for taking prompt military action. At first The Times had dismissed legal doubts about military intervention as "quibbles"; but, as bipartisan political support for military intervention began to evaporate, the "quibbles" became more important. Monckton's doubts about the legality of military intervention without another hostile act by President Nasser were shared by Sir Gerald Fitzmaurice, the Foreign Office's Senior Legal Advisor.

Those who believed that *Operation Musketeer* could be launched without further provocation were supported by a letter to the Times on August 11th from Professor Arthur Goodhart, the former Professor of Jurisprudence at Oxford and the Editor of the *Law Quarterly Review*, who wrote:

"It has been said that under modern international law, force must never be used except to repel a direct territorial attack. This view cannot be accepted as the use of force is not so limited; thus, for example, a State may take all necessary steps to protect the lives of its citizens abroad. Similarly, it may use force to protect a vital national interest which has been imperilled. In such a case it is the State that has altered the Status Quo by the use of force which is guilty of aggression." Professor Goodhart's letter was much quoted by Ministers. But it was not enough. By the end of August, there was general opinion, inside and outside Government, that a new *Casus Belli* would be needed to start military action.

The most vociferous doubter about the wisdom of using force was still the President of the United States. On September 2nd he wrote another letter to the Prime Minister: " ..... I regard it as indispensable that if we are to proceed solidly together to the solution of this problem, public opinion in our several countries must be overwhelmingly in its support. I must tell you frankly that American public opinion flatly rejects the thought of using force ..... I really do not see how a successful result could be achieved by forcible means. The use of force would, it seems to me, vastly increase the area of jeopardy. I do not see how the economy of Western Europe can long survive the burden of prolonged military operations, as well as the denial of Near East oil. Also, the people of the Near East and of North Africa and, to some extent, of all of Asia and all of Africa, would be consolidated against the West to a degree which, I fear could not be overcome in a generation and, perhaps, not even in a century ....."

Anthony Eden replied on September 6th and once again reminded the President of the errors of pre-war appeasement: "In the 1930s, Hitler established his position by a series of carefully planned movements. These began with the occupation of the Rhineland and were followed by successive acts of aggression against Austria, Czechoslovakia, Poland and the West. His actions were tolerated and excused by the majority of the population of Western Europe. It was argued either that Hitler had committed no act of aggression against anyone or that he was entitled to do what he liked in his own territory or that it was impossible to prove that he had any ulterior designs or that the covenant of the League of Nations did not entitle us to use force and that it would be wiser to wait until he did commit an act of aggression .....

"Similarly, the seizure of the Suez Canal is, we are convinced, the opening gambit in a planned campaign designed by Nasser to expel all Western influence and interests from Arab countries. He believes that if he can get away with this and, if he can successfully defy eighteen nations, his prestige in Arabia will be so great that he will be able to mount revolutions of young Officers in Saudi Arabia, Jordan, Syria and Iraq. (We know from our joint sources that he is already preparing a revolution in Iraq which is the most stable and progressive.) These new governments will in effect be Egyptian satellites if not Russian ones. They will have to place their united oil resources under the control of a united Arabia led by Egypt and under Russian influence. When that moment comes, Nasser can deny oil to Western Europe and we here shall all be at his mercy."

On September 25th, Harold Macmillan had a half hour discussion with President Eisenhower in the White House. As Chancellor of the Exchequer, he was visiting America for a meeting of the International Monetary Fund. President Eisenhower's opposition to the use of force seemed to be unshakable; but Harold Macmillan formed a rather different opinion after their conversation. As Harold Macmillan noted in his diary, "on Suez, he was sure that we must get Nasser down. The only thing was how to do it. I made it quite clear that we could *not* play it long without aid on a very large scale – that is if playing it long involved buying dollar oil." Macmillan's interpretation of the President's views seems to have been distorted by a linguistic misunderstanding. When Macmillan referred to his country being prepared to go down "with bands playing and flags flying," Eisenhower did not understand that this meant using force.

Macmillan noted that the President went on to discuss the United Nations. As Eisenhower said, "we had created something which was all very well as long as we could control it. But soon, we might not be able to do so, even when we acted together. Anyway U.S. had to pay a big price - in economic aid etc. - for U.N. votes. What would happen in the next few years alarmed him. Why could not U.S., U.K., Germany and France form a group and try to settle all these things ahead of time - before they reached crisis stage".

CASCU or SCUA

While he was on holiday in Canada at the beginning of September, Dulles produced a new scheme for handling the Canal crisis if Nasser rejected the proposals of the London Conference. The principal countries whose ships used the Canal would form an Association which would hire the pilots and organise the traffic through the Canal from Headquarters' ships which would be stationed at each end of the Canal. The Association would collect the dues from the ships that used their pilots.

Would it work? Was it meant to work? As Dulles noted on September 8th, "I showed the President the draft outline of a plan for a Users Association. The President went though this and said that he thought it was interesting but was not sure that it would work. I said that I was not sure either."

On September 15th, while the idea of SCUA was being discussed, many of the old Canal Company's non-Egyptian pilots walked out. This move had been encouraged by some of the former directors. The Egyptian pilots, helped by their Greek colleagues, managed to steer a particularly large number of ships safely through the Canal. It was no longer possible to argue that, in the short-term, the Egyptian authorities could not manage this important international waterway.

There was a wide-spread suspicion that Dulles had produced his scheme in order to enmesh those who wanted to use force; but, one of the more outspoken critics of the Dulles scheme was the Leader of the Opposition. When Parliament was recalled for a two day debate beginning on September 12th, Gaitskell said that the setting up of SCUA, "seems to me to be dangerously like a highly provocative act." Some of the practical problems inherent in SCUA were outlined in the debate by Richard Crossman, one of the Opposition's Foreign Affairs spokesmen. "I am exceedingly interested in SCUA. That is because I live near the Midland Railway. I take it that when the Midland Railway was nationalised ..... I would have been entitled to set up a Users Committee of those who disliked nationalisation and to say that we would collect the ticket fees in protest."

Discussion of the practicalities of SCUA, however, played only a small part in the September debate. In the debate on August 2nd almost every speaker on both sides of the House called for swift and firm action. On September 12th and 13th, however, almost every Opposition speaker had accused the Prime Minister of wanting war and of failing to take the dispute to the United Nations. On September 13th, the Labour Party's spokesman on Foreign Affairs, Alfred Robens, had moved an official Labour Party amendment which said:
"While condemning the arbitrary methods employed by the Egyptian government in respect of the Suez Canal Company and resolved to support the legitimate rights of the users of the Canal, deplores the refusal of Her Majesty's Government to refer the dispute immediately to the United Nations, to declare that they will not use force except in conformity with our obligations under the Charter of the United Nations and to refrain meanwhile from any form of provocative action."

As Selwyn Lloyd, the Foreign Secretary, responded, "My sorrow in this debate is that the Leader of the Opposition has yielded to the temptation of trying to use a grave international situation for Party advantage. If the position of this country has been weakened, that is what has weakened it ..... we are not prepared to let unrestricted control of the operation of this Canal pass into the hands of one government or of one man and upon that issue we are not prepared to compromise."

At a press conference which he called on September 13th, Dulles made it plain that the American government would not to try to coerce Egypt into accepting the proposed plan if the Egyptians blocked SCUA. "We do not intend to shoot our way through," Dulles went on to say, "the American government would advise ships to go round the Cape of Good Hope." In the first fortnight of its embryonic existence, the Suez Canal Users Association had been transformed by its principal parent into the Cape of Good Hope Shipping Association.

Going to the United Nations

On September 19th, Selwyn Lloyd was elected Chairman of another Suez Conference. This was to discuss the setting up of SCUA. Thirteen of the eighteen countries that had supported the Menzies mission to Nasser sent their Foreign Ministers. There was some discussion about the title of the organisation. It had first been called CASCU (the Cooperative Association of Suez Canal Users). This, unfortunately, turned out to mean something obscene in Portuguese. Other combinations of initials could not be used in polite society in Turkey. SCUA, however, seemed acceptable in every language.

Behind the scenes at the Conference there was much discussion about the United Nations. Almost everyone, it seemed, wanted a reference to the U.N. as soon as possible. On the final day of the Conference, Selwyn Lloyd had given a lunch for the Representatives of Iran, New Zealand, Norway and Portugal. All were in favour of going to the United Nations. The principal opponent of taking the United Nations route had been the American Secretary of State. A wide-ranging debate on nationalisation would have been a potential source of much embarrassment for the American government. In any U.N. debate, the Soviet Union would have loudly championed Nasser's nationalisation, which had been so popular in the Middle East. The American spokesman would have to choose between making a speech supporting the rising tide of Arab nationalism or of standing by its traditional allies, Great Britain and France.

The British government had also been understandably reluctant to get drawn into "the quicksand" of United Nations procedure. Without firm American backing there might well be a United Nations vote condemning the use of force. The dispute would go first to the Security Council which would probably be sympathetic if the Americans played a constructive role. Apart from the five permanent Members: Britain, France, China, the Soviet Union and the United States, the Security Council in 1956 consisted of: Australia, Belgium, Cuba, Iran, Peru, and Yugoslavia. In the past year, however, there had been a dramatic change in the membership of the U.N. General Assembly. In 1945 there had been 50 original Members of the United Nations; ten years later, in 1955, there were still only 60 countries represented in the Assembly: but in the last year, that number had increased dramatically to 79; and most of the new Members were 'third world' countries that might be expected to side instinctively with the Egyptians.

While Dulles was still calling for delay, the Foreign Secretary sent a letter to the President of the Security Council asking for a meeting of the Council on Wednesday, September 26th to discuss "the situation created by the unilateral action of the Egyptian government in bringing to an end the system of international operation of the Suez Canal which was confirmed by the Suez Canal Convention of 1888".

The discussions at the United Nations went more smoothly than might have been expected. A general debate on October the 8th and 9th was followed by private meetings between the Secretary General Dag Hammarskjöld and the Foreign Ministers of Great Britain, France and Egypt. They produced a set of six principals which were remarkably similar to the proposals put forward in August at the first London Canal Users Conference: (1) that there should be free and open transit through the Canal without discrimination, overt or covert; (2) that there should be respect for Egyptian sovereignty; (3) that the operation of the Canal should be insulated from the politics of any country; (4) that the level of dues should be fixed by agreement between users and owners; (5) that a fair proportion of the dues should be allotted to development and (6) that disputes between the Suez Canal

Company and the Egyptian government should be settled by arbitration with suitable terms of reference and suitable provision for the payment of the sums found to be due.

These six principals were supported by all eleven members of the Security Council but how were they to be implemented? The Soviet Union vetoed the Anglo-French proposal on how the principals should be enforced. Progress had been made; but it looked as though many weeks of discussion about implementation lay ahead. After the Security Council vote, President Eisenhower spoke at a press conference. "I have got the best announcement that I could make to America tonight. The progress made in the settlement of the Suez dispute this afternoon at the United Nations is most gratifying. Egypt, Britain and France have met through their Foreign Ministers and agreed on a set of principals on which to negotiate and it looks like there is a very great crisis that is behind us." Selwyn Lloyd immediately protested. As Selwyn Lloyd now cabled to Anthony Eden, the endorsement of the six principals by the Security Council was a positive step forward. On the debit side, however, Nasser was still in control; and the next round of negotiations might go on for the rest of the year.

Marching as to War

Christian Pineau, the French Foreign Minister, had been a depressed observer of the British political scene for many weeks. In the days that followed Nasser's nationalisation it had looked as though "strong and resolute" action would be taken. Now, British resolution and British strength seemed to be ebbing away. If Great Britain would not take part in the war that France was already fighting against Nasser in Algeria, could the Israelis take their place?

By September 21st, Pineau was sure that the British would not start military action against Egypt. As he left London after Ministerial talks, Pineau told the British Prime Minister that France might act alone - and even be aided by Israel. Eden's reply, according to Pineau, was that he was not opposed to this plan as long as Israel did not attack Jordan. In the two months after nationalisation there had been several Franco-Israeli Staff talks; but now the Foreign Minister of France was proposing something much more serious. He was suggesting that Israel should go to war against Egypt as an ally of France. This would have to be discussed at the highest political level.

On September 28th an Israeli Delegation led by Golda Meir, the new Israeli Foreign Minister, and including both Moshe Dayan and Shimon Peres, flew to Paris where they met Christian Pineau, Maurice Bourgès-Maunoury, the French Minister of Defence, and General Challe, a Deputy Chief of Staff.

Pineau began by asking whether Israel was interested in taking military action against Egypt if Great Britain would not take part. If Israel was prepared to act, the French would give Israel all possible military aid and full political backing in the Security Council using France's veto whenever necessary. Either, Israel could launch the action on her own and then France would send in her forces or, the two countries could act together. Pineau said that the most suitable date for military action was sometime before the middle of October. There would be storms in the Mediterranean later and he thought that the action should begin during the American Presidential campaign.

In her reply, Golda Meir agreed that there was now no alternative to military action; but Israel had to be sure that Britain would not help Jordan if Jordan helped Egypt. There was a danger that Israel might find herself fighting with France against Egypt; and also against Great Britain and Jordan. The Israelis were particularly anxious about the American reaction. If America declared an economic embargo there would be grave hardship in Israel.

What would the British do? As Dayan noted: "The most desirable development for Britain would be an Israeli attack on Egypt. She could then rush to Egypt's defence and drive out Israel's forces and, since British troops would then find themselves in the Suez area, they would automatically stay to control the Canal ..... The British wanted France to be an insulated link with Israel. Through France, they would get us to do what was desirable for Britain while guaranteeing them freedom from contact with Israel."

There was some discussion about the Israeli battle plans. The Israeli Army would drive towards the Canal, by-passing the Egyptian fortified defensive positions. Some paratroopers would be dropped behind the Egyptian lines. Every effort would be made to confuse the Egyptian High Command. They would reach the Canal in five to seven days.

When the Israeli delegation flew home they were accompanied by a French military mission. Unexpectedly, Ben-Gurion seemed doubtful about the whole operation. In January 1956, Ben-Gurion had actually proposed a unilateral military assault to break the blockade of the Straits of Tiran; but he now seemed obsessed with the amount of damage that the Egyptian Air Force could do to Israeli cities. He had lived in London during part of the German blitz. Ben-Gurion feared that if the Israelis did attack Egypt, they would be opposed, diplomatically and physically, by a British government that would welcome an opportunity to pose as the defender of the Arabs. Ben-Gurion had many unhappy memories of negotiating with British governments. Before World War II he had taken part in the discussions that preceded the imposition of a drastic reduction in the rate of Jewish immigration into Palestine. After World War II, Ben-Gurion had watched with dismay as the 1945 Labour government had maintained the rigid restriction on the number of Jews allowed to enter Palestine - despite the fact that the Labour Party had spent many years during the war calling for a pro-Jewish immigration policy.

Dayan hoped that Ben-Gurion would agree to fight with France as an ally. He had argued that it would be folly to reject the French offer of an alliance. As Dayan pointed out, neither the British nor the French needed military help to defeat the Egyptians. "The sole quality we possess ..... and they lacked, was the ability to supply the necessary pretext. This alone could provide us with a ticket of admission to the Suez Canal Club ..... If France were willing to undertake joint action with us, it would be in the highest degree unfortunate if we rejected their offer and returned to our state of isolated struggle." Ben-Gurion was still unimpressed by the idea that Israel should start the war by attacking Egypt so that the French and the British could tell the Israelis to stop. Israel was being asked "to mount the rostrum of shame", as he put it, so that Great Britain and France "could wash their hands in the waters of purity".

Getting Together?

On October 14th Anthony Eden was resting at Chequers, the Prime Minister's country home, after the Conservative Party Conference. His speech there had been warmly applauded; but there seemed to be very little hope that the Foreign Secretary would return from his negotiations at the United Nations with the sort of agreement that would satisfy a Conservative Conference.

The latest report from the Joint intelligence Committee also made gloomy reading. At the beginning of August, the J.I.C. had predicted that, if there was an uncertain result after discussions at the United Nations, Soviet influence on Egypt would increase. In mid-October, the J.I.C. had repeated that prediction; and it seemed highly likely that Nasser would emerge unscathed from the U.N. discussions.

There were also problems with Jordan. In 1955, the number of Israelis killed in Fedayeen attacks had exceeded 200 in that year. Many of these lethal attacks had been launched from Jordan. There had also been a sharp increase in the number of Israeli retaliatory raids.

As Prime Minister of Israel, Ben-Gurion fervently believed that the Israeli State had a moral duty to be seen to avenge the deaths of its citizens. After the Holocaust, he believed that the people who killed Jews should be punished. This view was shared by Moshe Dayan, who became Chief of Staff of the Israeli Defence Force at the end of 1953. Dayan also believed that retaliatory raids provided excellent training for young officers and N.C.O.s in his Army.

This decision not to turn the other cheek did not win Israel many friends at the United Nations. The murder of an Israeli mother and her baby, or the killing of a couple of Israeli students, hardly ever attracted international attention but an Israeli Army raid on a Jordanian police station or an Egyptian army camp would quickly lead to a complaint at Security Council.

On October 10th, the Israeli Army launched a particularly strong assault on an Arab Legion fort near Qalqilya. There were heavy casualties on both sides; 18 Israeli soldiers (including eight Officers) were killed.

During the fighting at Qalqilya, the King of Jordan had asked the British Headquarters on Cyprus for help under the Anglo-Jordan Defence Treaty. On October 11th, the British Chargé d'Affaires in Tel Aviv told the Israeli Prime Minister that an Iraqi division was about to enter Jordan; and that British Forces would help Jordan if the Israelis took military action. The British Headquarters already had detailed plans - *Operation Cordage* - for naval and aerial action against Israel. As the situation on the Jordanian frontier deteriorated, Jewish members of the British armed forces serving in the Middle East were quietly sent home.

While Anthony Eden was contemplating the possibility of war with Israel, he was visited at Chequers by Albert Gazier and Major-General Maurice Challe. Albert Gazier, who was the French Minister for Social Affairs was acting for Christian Pineau, the French Foreign Minister who was at the United Nations Headquarters in New York. Maurice Challe had played a leading role in the French discussions with Israel. He had been awarded a D.S.O. in 1944 for leading a spectacular operation for the French Resistance which gave the Allies important information about the deployment of the Luftwaffe on the eve of D-Day.

After a brief discussion about the dangerous tension on the Israeli-Jordan truce line, Gazier asked what Britain would do if Israel attacked Egypt. Challe then talked about a new idea for launching *Musketeer*. Israel would invade Egypt; and after a short pause, Britain and France would intervene as peacemakers in order to separate the combatants. Both the Israelis and the

Egyptians would be ordered to withdraw from the Canal. When the Egyptians refused, their airfields would be bombed and the Anglo-French force would land at Port Said. Under the Challe plan.

Nasser might be defeated without alienating Britain's Arab allies. It was clearly an idea that had to be discussed by Eden and Lloyd with Mollet and Pineau.

In 1944, Challe had helped the Allies invade France. Twelve years later, he was helping to launch another invasion.

Consultation, Cooperation or Collusion?

On October 21st, a French aircraft carried Ben-Gurion, Dayan and Shimon Peres to Paris for talks with the French "war cabinet" - Guy Mollet, The Prime Minister, Christian Pineau, the Foreign Minister, and Maurice Bourgès-Maunoury, the Defence Minister. A senior British Cabinet Minister would join them later at Sevrès, in the outskirts of Paris.

A thick cloud over the Parisian airfields delayed the arrival of the Israelis and a thick cloud of Israeli caution hung over the conference. Ben-Gurion did not like the details of the Challe scenario that had been presented to Anthony Eden at Chequers. It was now proposed that there would be a 72-hour gap between the Israeli invasion of the Sinai and the Anglo-French intervention. This would leave Israel exposed to diplomatic attack from all sides at the United Nations. Israel would also be vulnerable to bombs dropped by the Egyptian IL.28 aircraft until proper attacks could be made on Egyptian airfields. The main cloud in Ben-Gurion's mind, however, was his suspicion of British intentions. Would the British turn on the Israelis if there was an attack in Sinai?

The arrival of Selwyn Lloyd did not allay Israeli anxieties. Selwyn Lloyd was brusque and unfriendly. His opening remarks about the substantial progress of the negotiations at the United Nations were a reminder that the Foreign Office never forgot the over-riding importance of supporting Britain's Arab friends in the Middle East.

Selwyn Lloyd made it plain that the British would not be able to intervene to "protect the Canal" unless the Israelis opened the conflict with a "real act of war" near the Suez Canal. Ben-Gurion repeated his opposition to the idea that Israel should stand alone as an aggressor; but he now called on Dayan to put forward an alternative scenario. The Israeli military plan was designed to confuse the Egyptians. Wherever possible, the Israelis would go round Egyptian strong points during their advance toward the Canal and would attack them from the rear. The Israeli Army could make their first assault look like a reprisal raid to the Egyptians rather than a "real act of war". It was unlikely that the Egyptians would bomb Tel Aviv or Haifa in response to a large reprisal raid. The original Israeli plan had called for the dropping of a couple of parachute platoons quite close to the Canal in order to carry out some diversionary attacks. Now the Israelis offered to expand their airborne activity by dropping a battalion close to the Canal. It was not a very large alteration to the plan; but the Dayan formula seemed to satisfy Selwyn Lloyd. The Foreign Secretary also seemed prepared to cut the time that would elapse between the Israeli attack and the delivery of an Anglo-French ultimatum to both the Israelis and the Egyptians. Both countries would be ordered to withdraw ten miles from the Canal.

Both Dayan and Peres, who had been the principal architect of the massive French arms shipments to Israel, were desperately anxious that Ben-Gurion should not reject the French plan. France was the only ally that Israel could count upon. As Bourgès-Maunoury quietly pointed out, if Israel did not play her part by invading Egypt now, there would be no possibility in the future of joint Franco-Israeli operations. The French were also prepared to reduce Ben-Gurion's anxieties about Egyptian bombs by agreeing to station a re-enforced squadron of Mystère IV's on Israeli airfields before the fighting began.

Of course, the proposed ultimatum was not even-handed. The Israelis were not asked to retreat behind their own frontier with Egypt. They were not even asked to withdraw from any position that they were likely to occupy. Meanwhile, the Egyptians would be told to pull back their forces from their own territory. Even the most skilful lawyers would find it difficult to refute the inevitable allegation that there had been collusion or, at least, joint consultation.

There was also no doubt that the French wanted to start the operation as quickly as possible. Dayan suggested that October 29th was the earliest date on which the Israelis would be ready to move. Pineau gave three reasons for moving so quickly. After the beginning of November, bad weather might add to the problems. It would also be difficult to keep the French strike force in a high state of readiness beyond the end of October.

For Pineau, however, the main political argument in favour of October 29th was the fact that it came just before the American presidential election on November 6th. It was hardly surprising that Pineau thought that this was a good idea. In the last few months, Dulles had often told his fellow Foreign Ministers that America would not be able to take any major initiative about the Middle East shortly before a presidential election because of the importance of the Jewish vote. In a special election in 1949, Dulles had run for the Senate from the state of New York. His opponent had been the former Governor, Herbert Lehman, who was the most effective Jewish politician in the state. Dulles had been badly beaten.

Once again, Ben-Gurion struck a discordant note. Would the Americans be told about this plan? Israel was anxious not to alienate the American government. If there was serious disagreement, Israel would be particularly vulnerable to American economic pressure. And what about the Soviet Union? In the three months since Nasser had nationalised the Canal, the Soviet leaders had been preoccupied with political problems in Poland and political violence in Hungary. As their trauma in Hungary was reaching a violent climax, the Soviet Union might want to flex its military muscles by sending volunteers to use the weapons that had already been delivered to Egypt. Guy Mollet and Selwyn Lloyd could tell Ben-Gurion when they would begin to bomb Egyptian airfields but there were no sensible answers to Ben-Gurion's questions about the Americans and the Russians.

Selwyn Lloyd returned to London shortly before midnight. The French participants were worried that his report to Anthony Eden would be negative, and Pineau flew after him to make sure that the Challe scenario was still on track. In fact, parliamentary duties would make it difficult for Selwyn Lloyd to return to Sèvres for a final session. His place was taken by Patrick Dean, the Chairman of the J.I.C., and Donald Logan, Selwyn Lloyd's Private Secretary who had attended the first round of talks.

It was clear that some written record of the important decisions should be made. While Dean and Logan waited, a document was typed out in French:

THE PROTOCOL

On the afternoon of October 29th Israeli Forces would launch a full-scale attack on the Egyptian forces.

On October 30th the British and French governments would appeal to Egypt for an absolute ceasefire, the withdrawal of forces to ten miles from the Canal and acceptance of the temporary occupation of the key positions on the Canal by Anglo-French forces.

There would, simultaneously, be an appeal to the government of Israel for an absolute ceasefire and a withdrawal of forces to 10 miles east of the Canal. If either of the two governments rejected the appeal, or failed to give its agreement within twelve hours, the Anglo-French forces would intervene; if the Egyptians refused, the Anglo-French forces would attack early on October 31st.

Israel agreed not to attack Jordan. But if Jordan attacked Israel Britain would not go to Jordan's assistance as the Anglo-Jordanian treaty refers specifically to the defence of Jordan against Israeli (or other) attack.

Israeli forces would seize the western shore of the Gulf of Aqaba and insure control of the Gulf of Tiran.

Anthony Eden was upset when he heard that Patrick Dean had signed a document *ad referendum* – which meant that his signature was only valid when approved by his government. Dean and Logan were immediately flown back to Paris in order to try and destroy this written record. The Israelis had already gone home with their copy and the French would not hand over their papers. At Sèvres, there had been an agreement that the details of the discussion should remain secret forever. Selwyn Lloyd had travelled to Paris wearing an anonymous raincoat. He was supposed to be at home suffering from a bad cold. Clearly the British government had most to lose if it became known that there had been serious military discussions with the Israelis.

Who Should Be Told?

Who could be told and who should be told about the plan? Clearly, common sense suggested that the number of people aware of what was going to happen should be tightly restricted. Telling large numbers of people that Israel was about to attack Egypt could be damaging militarily and politically; but British troops could hardly be sent into action without the approval of the Cabinet.

On October 23rd, while Selwyn Lloyd was still engaged at Sèvres, Eden told his Cabinet colleagues:

"It now seemed unlikely that the Israelis would launch a full-scale attack against Egypt. The United Kingdom and French governments were thus confronted with the choice between an early military operation or a relatively prolonged negotiation. If the second course were followed, neither we, nor the French, could hope to maintain our military preparations in their present state of readiness ..... The French government were seriously concerned at this possibility and were disposed to favour earlier military action ..... They would not, however, be in a position to take such action effectively unless we gave them facilities to operate from Cyprus, and it was possible that they might press us to grant those facilities."

On October 24th, the Cabinet met again. The French Government had just withdrawn their Ambassador from Cairo following the interception of *S.S. Athos*, a Sudanese registered ship loaded with 70 tons of Egyptian weapons meant for the Algerian rebels. The Cabinet was told that the French "were unwilling to use the gun-running incident as a ground for taking military action against Egypt ..... while they favoured early military action they were unable to find any sufficient grounds for undertaking it at the present time."

According to the minutes: "the Cabinet were informed that the military operation which had been planned could not be held in readiness for many days longer. There was growing dissatisfaction among the reservists who had been recalled for service, and it would be difficult to retain them for much longer unless there was some significant development in the Suez dispute, by which they could be convinced that their services would soon be required. Moreover, the condition of the vehicles which had been loaded in merchant ships for many weeks was now deteriorating, and the time was fast approaching when they would have to be unloaded and serviced. For both these reasons, the military authorities would prefer to adopt, after the end of October, a new military plan which could be held in readiness to be put into operation, at about 14 days notice, at any time throughout the winter. Under this plan, the reservists would be released, and again recalled when a fresh emergency arose; and the vehicles would be unloaded from merchant ships and, for the most part, stored on land. It would be difficult to switch over to this winter plan without giving the public the impression that our military precautions were being relaxed. This could not fail to weaken our bargaining position in any negotiations which were undertaken with the Egyptian government on the Suez Canal issue."

In the discussion that followed the Prime Minister was asked whether a military operation would unite the Arab world in support of Egypt. The Prime Minister then said: "This was a serious risk; but against it must be set the greater risk that, unless early action could be taken to damage Colonel

Nasser's prestige, his influence would be extended throughout the Middle East to a degree which would make it much more difficult to overthrow him. It was known that he was already plotting coups in many of the other Arab countries; and we should never have a better pretext for intervention against him than we had now as a result of his seizure of the Suez Canal. If, however, a military operation were undertaken against Egypt, its effect in other Arab countries would be serious unless it led to the early collapse of Colonel Nasser's regime. Both for this reason and also because of the international pressures which would develop ..... it must be quick and successful."

After a brief discussion of the risks facing British citizens in Arab countries: " the Cabinet then considered the prospects of bringing the Suez issue to a head by diplomatic means. The Egyptians might be asked to produce, within a specified time limit, their alternative proposals for placing the Canal under international supervision. This course would be in conformity with the Security Council Resolution. It was, however, open to two objections. First, the French would not welcome an early resumption of the negotiations with Egypt. Secondly, if such a demand were made, the Egyptians were likely to comply with it – by producing within the specified time – proposals which, though unsatisfactory, would appear to afford a basis for discussion. In that event, a breaking point could only be reached after several days of discussion. If therefore, the Cabinet chose the course of negotiation, they would face a dilemma. They could frame their demands in such a way as to make it impossible for the Egyptians to accept them – being resolved, on an Egyptian refusal, to take military action designed to overthrow Colonel Nasser's regime. Alternatively they could seek the sort of settlement of the Canal issue which might be reached by negotiation – recognising that, by accepting such a settlement, they would abandon their ..... objective of reducing Colonel Nasser's influence throughout the Middle East."

In summing up the discussion, the Prime Minister said that: "Before their final decision was taken, further discussions with the French government would be required."

When the cabinet did meet again on October 25th, the situation had changed dramatically. It was now clear that the Israelis were going to attack Egypt. As the Prime Minister told the Cabinet: "They evidently felt that the ambitions of Colonel Nasser's government threatened their continued existence as an independent state and that they could not afford to wait for others to curb his expansionist policies. The Cabinet must therefore consider the situation which was likely to arise if hostilities broke out between Israel and Egypt."

"The French government were strongly of the view that intervention would be justified in order to limit the hostilities and that for this purpose it would be right to launch the military operation against Egypt which had already been mounted. Indeed, it was possible that if we declined to join them, they would take military action alone or in conjunction with Israel. In these circumstances the Prime Minister suggested that, if Israel launched a full-scale military operation against Egypt the governments of the United Kingdom and France, should at once call on both parties to stop hostilities and to withdraw their forces to a distance of ten miles from the Canal; and that it should at the same time be made clear that, if one or both governments failed to undertake within twelve hours to comply with these requirements, British and French forces would intervene in order to enforce compliance. Israel might well undertake to comply with such a demand. If Egypt also complied, Nasser's prestige would be fatally undermined. If she failed to comply there would be ample justification for Anglo-French military action against Egypt in order to safeguard the Canal. We must face the risk that we should be accused of collusion with Israel. But this charge was liable to be brought against us in any event; for it could now be assumed that, if an Anglo-French operation were undertaken against Egypt, we should be unable to prevent the Israelis from launching a parallel attack themselves; and it was preferable that we should be seen to be holding the balance between Israel and Egypt rather than appear to be accepting Israeli cooperation in an attack on Egypt alone."

There was a sharp intake of breath from some Cabinet Ministers; but no outright opposition or threat of resignation – even from Walter Monckton who had recently moved from the Ministry of Defence to a sinecure position in the Cabinet as Paymaster General.

There were many questions. Could Britain really claim to be holding any sort of balance between Israel and Egypt? And what about the Americans?

The terms of the ultimatum meant that there was no way in which the Prime Minister could avoid the charge that Britain was not being even-handed; clearly, the Americans would be upset if they were not told. However, President Eisenhower had often said that he was opposed to using force; and, if he were to be given advance information, he might be able to stop the whole operation by putting public pressure on Israel.

No one raised the question of whether it would be more sensible to postpone the operation for one week until the American election was over.

There were obvious difficulties about telling other Ministers outside the Cabinet about the conflict before it began. When Anthony Eden had first been told about the "Challe scenario" at Chequers, he was sitting next to Anthony Nutting, the Minister of State at the Foreign Office. Anthony Nutting, who had just delivered a bellicose speech at the Conservative Party Conference, was upset by what he heard. When Selwyn Lloyd flew back from the United Nations 48 hours later, Nutting tried unsuccessfully to persuade the Foreign Secretary that he should oppose the plan. Nutting failed; but, before he resigned from the Government, Nutting briefed two other Foreign Office Ministers, Lord Reading and Douglas Dodds-Parker. Curiously, these Foreign Office Ministers received no guidance about Sèvres from Selwyn Lloyd, although, in the next few days, they would have to answer questions in Parliament.

Fortunately for the Prime Minister Sir Ivone Kirkpatrick, the official head of the Foreign Service, supported the "Challe scenario" but the question of which officials and which ambassadors could be told was a problem that caused much anxiety. Very few members of the Foreign Office's Middle East department could be expected to approve of marching in step with Israel; but very few officials needed to know.

Telling the Commanders

It was, of course, going to be necessary to change *Musketeer Revise*, the latest of the many alterations in the military plan which had been prepared by the Chiefs of Staff in August. From the beginning, there had been unhappiness about the number of Egyptian civilian casualties that would be caused by air and sea bombardment before any landing. Even natural hawks like Lord Hailsham, who had become First Lord of the Admiralty at the beginning of September, sought ways of reducing the inevitable collateral damage. After Sèvres, this became a political as well as a humanitarian imperative.

Unfortunately, the final version of *Musketeer Revise* had called for five days of intensive aero-psycho bombardment after the destruction of the Egyptian Air force. Of course, the bombing campaign would be directed at targets outside towns and cities. Cairo Radio was an obvious target once it had been confirmed that the transmitter was not located in the middle of Cairo. There would, however, be a steady assault on military and economic targets throughout Egypt; and Egyptians would be constantly reminded by broadcasts and pamphlets dropped from the air, that they were vulnerable to a heavy assault. If Britain was really trying to separate two armies, bombing Egyptian civilians - or even threatening to bomb Egyptian civilians - would be politically calamitous. Before Sèvres, "shock and awe" might well have been a sensible strategy. After Sèvres, a massive campaign to frighten ordinary Egyptians made no sense at all. Anthony Head, the new Minister of Defence, was sent flying to Cyprus to explain that "shock and awe" had been abandoned and that the Anglo-French landing must be supported by minimal naval and air bombardment.

Which military Commanders, if any, should be told the real reason for the change of plan and what other changes should be made? The French were more relaxed about informing their military Commanders. On October 26th, General Stockwell met General Beaufre on the French airfield at Villacoublay where his French Deputy told the Land Force Commander about the new plan. General Stockwell's Chief of Staff now rang the British Embassy in Paris and asked them to send a message to London telling the rest of their Headquarter's staff to move to Cyprus quickly. General Stockwell then flew to Malta where he briefed the staff of Admiral Sir Guy Grantham, the Naval Commander, about the new scenario. At the beginning of August, General Stockwell had been ordered not to tell the French officers about British plans because of poor French security. At the end of October, British military and naval staffs got their knowledge of the new scenario from a briefing by General Beaufre. If the Israeli assault was as successful as the French seemed to think that it would be, it might be possible to speed up the whole operation.

What was needed was flexibility; but there was little room for flexibility in the detailed plans that had been drawn up for launching a mini D-Day. While Eden and Mollet were thinking of Munich and pre-war appeasement, the generals had recreated a World War II battle. When the Israeli soldiers cut through the Egyptian Army in the Sinai, the French called for a swift air and sea assault on the Canal zone using the Anglo-French forces already based on Cyprus. Once the Egyptian Air force had been eliminated, the aircraft carriers were not needed for the protection of the convoy against air attack. The carriers could have steamed forward to Port Said; and the slower ships in the convoy could have been left to look after themselves. An enthusiastic Mountbatten might have provided the driving force that was needed to speed up the landing; but the First Sea Lord was still writing letters of anxious protest about the whole operation, while General Keightley's natural caution made him reluctant to move quickly.

Into Battle

At 3:00 pm on Monday, October 29th, four Israeli-piloted Mustangs flew over the Israeli- Egyptian Armistice line and cut the main Egyptian Army telephone wires across Sinai with their wings and their propellers. At 5:20 pm, sixteen Dakotas dropped 395 paratroopers at the eastern end of the Mitla Pass. Some French aircraft, flying from Cyprus, soon dropped some special anti-tank weapons at the Mitla Pass as this equipment could not be loaded on to Israeli aircraft.

Less than twelve hours later, President Eisenhower called together a conference of his closest advisors at the White House. For days American Intelligence had been reporting on the size of the Israeli mobilisation and had noted the substantial increase in cable traffic between France and Israel. The C.I.A. and the State Department had thought that the Israeli's were preparing for a substantial assault on Jordan.

As the memorandum of the White House conference recorded, President Eisenhower was infuriated. It looked as though the Israelis had decided to attack just before the election because they thought that President Eisenhower would be reluctant to alienate the Jewish vote by taking action against them.

"The President recalled that in 1950 and later, we have said we would support the victim of aggression in the Middle East. The question now is, how shall we do this? ..... The President thought that in these circumstances perhaps we cannot be bound by our traditional alliances, but must instead face the question of how to make good on our pledge. He thought the UN might be the most valuable course to follow ..... The President said that, in this matter, he does not care in the slightest whether he is re-elected or not. He feels we must make good on our word. He added that he did not really think the American people would throw him out in the midst of a situation like this, but if they did so be it."

It was surprising that the President should attach so much importance to the 1950 Tripartite agreement. On March 18th, at the time of General Glubb's dismissal, Anthony Eden had written a letter to the President saying: *"I am becoming increasingly worried at the absence of any definite Anglo-American plan for dealing with aggression from either side in the Arab-Israel dispute. We should both be in a position of the up-most embarrassment if an attack occurred and we had to confess that in spite of all we have said about the Tripartite Declaration, no plan had been made for meeting it. I should be more than grateful for anything you can do to speed up the present talks."*

The talks had not, in fact, produced any sensible Tripartite plan. It would, of course, be easy enough to cripple Israel if Israel launched an attack. Her ports could be blockaded and her airfields demolished; but stopping an Arab attack on Israel would be much more difficult once the British garrison had been withdrawn from the Canal zone. The American plan for stopping an Egyptian attack on Israel consisted of dropping bombs on the Egyptian supply lines in Sinai. The British did not think much of the American plan. The British argued that the Tripartite Declaration could only be enforced if the Tripartite powers were ready and able to land a substantial force at Port Said. Unfortunately, neither the divisions nor the landing craft were in position. As the talks about updating the Tripartite moved slowly forward, President Eisenhower had shown some enthusiasm for loading a substantial quantity of modern weapons on board a ship and mooring the ship in the eastern Mediterranean. The weapons would be handed over to the victim of aggression. Clearly, this idea made no sense militarily and President Eisenhower must have been aware on October 29th that the Tripartite guarantees were of negligible value to Israel. Israeli Ministers had repeatedly pointed this out to the American Government once Soviet weapons had begun to pour in to Egypt.

President Eisenhower had not been impressed by these Israeli arguments. As Eisenhower's principle biographer, Stephen Ambrose, has written: "Eisenhower was uncomfortable with Jews ..... so much so, that he did not want to hear their side."

Even if President Eisenhower had been more sympathetic to Israeli anxieties, it would hardly have been surprising if he had felt personally embarrassed by the timing of the Israeli attack. President Eisenhower knew very well that, when he arrived in London in 1942 to take command of the Anglo-American Expeditionary Force that would soon invade North Africa, he was looked upon by many senior British Officers as a purely political General. In 1942, Anthony Eden had a more distinguished military record as a fighting

59

soldier than General Eisenhower. During World War I, young Eden had an exceptionally gallant record while serving in the trenches with the King's Royal Rifle Corps. He had won a Military Cross for saving his platoon Sergeant in no-man's land – an action that might well have won a recommendation for the Victoria Cross. In November 1918, Anthony Eden had become the youngest Brigade Major in the British Army.

Young Dwight Eisenhower, however, had not heard a shot fired in anger during World War I. In that conflict he had commanded a number of training establishments within the United States. General Eisenhower owed his swift promotion after 1939 to his work with General George Marshall, the exceptionally distinguished Army Chief of Staff. In 1940, 1941 and 1942, General Marshall, played a major role in the rapid strengthening of the American Army. Colonel Eisenhower had been General Marshall's right hand man. In June 1942, the newly promoted General Eisenhower arrived in England as Commander of all the American soldiers in the European Theatre of Operations. General Marshall had personally chosen Eisenhower for this post.

As many British senior Officers resented the fact that an American had been chosen to command the North African campaign and, as virtually all the senior British Generals had seen much active service during World War II, General Eisenhower was well aware that many of his British colleagues looked upon him as a political appointee rather than a proper fighting General.

After World War II, General Marshall had become the Secretary of State in President Truman's administration. Their only major disagreement had come in May 1948 when President Truman told him that he was going to recognise the State of Israel as soon as it had declared its independence. General Marshall did not agree. He accused President Truman of ignoring the national interest in a bid for the Jewish vote at the forthcoming presidential election. It was an unfair accusation; but General Marshall told President Truman that he would not vote for him again. Now, eight years later, it looked as though the British, the French and the Israelis believed that President Eisenhower would be prepared to manipulate American policy in order to secure the Jewish vote. It was a personal insult.

Bad Days for Ben-Gurion

At 4:30 p.m. on October 30th, an ultimatum was handed to the Egyptian Ambassador in London. Fifteen minutes earlier, the Israeli Ambassador had received a similar note.

While this diplomatic activity was taking place in London, the rest of Sharon's parachute brigade was getting close to linking up with the Israeli battalion that had dropped at the Mitla Pass. As Dayan had predicted, the rough desert terrain presented the main problem for the advancing soldiers. Sharon's brigade had started with 13 light tanks. Ten of these had broken down by the time that the Israelis attacked the first Egyptian strongpoint. The brigade should have started their advance with 153 of the French-supplied front-wheel-drive trucks. When they crossed the frontier, they had 46 of these vital vehicles and there were no tools for running repairs during their 150 mile advance.

Shortly before midnight, Sharon's brigade joined the Mitla battalion. Despite specific instructions that they should not try and capture the Pass, a substantial force of Sharon's men drove into the Pass and were soon involved in a fierce battle with the well-entrenched Egyptian defenders. After the fiercest hand-to-hand combat of the campaign, the Pass was cleared; but 38 Israelis were killed and 120 injured. On October 30th, the Egyptian Air force made 40 attacks on the advancing Israeli columns. On October 31st, there were 90 attacks. Four Egyptian aircraft were shot down.

On October 31st, Ben-Gurion was in bed with flu. The Egyptian air activity on October 30th had been expected; but, according to the Sèvres timetable, the Royal Air force should have begun to attack Egyptian airfields at dawn on October 31st. This did not happen. In the middle of the afternoon, Ben-Gurion sent a message to Bourgès Maunoury: "I am cast down and confused by the fact that at this hour we are still without news of an Anglo-French operation against the Egyptian airfields ..... The members of the Government are asking me if we have been abandoned to our fate."

Finally, at 4:15 p.m., Almaza airfield, near Cairo, was attacked. (There had been briefing problems and the RAF Commanders had not wanted to start the main bombing campaign in daylight.) In the next 48 hours, the Anglo-French bomber force dropped 1,962 bombs in 18 attacks on 13 targets. More than 220 Egyptian aircraft were destroyed.

While the first British bombers were approaching Almaza, Hugh Gaitskell was on his feet in the House of Commons. His message was clear:

"Hon. Members ..... may jeer at us and laugh at our faith in the United Nations and may rejoice ..... to be back in the days of the 19th century; but all this ..... will not stop the wave of hatred of Britain which they have stirred up ..... I must now tell the Government and the country that we cannot support the action they have taken and that we shall feel bound by every constitutional means at our disposal to oppose it."

The Leader of the Opposition's sharp words were not unexpected. On October 30th, Gaitskell had forced a division after an unusual debate in which the Government had defended Israel. As Selwyn Lloyd argued: "If a man has said that he is going to cut one's throat, is it an act of aggression if one kicks the knife out of his hand? ..... We must remember the facts of the situation and that ..... Israel is the next target. " Hugh Gaitskell was a well-known friend of Israel whose recent election as Leader of the Labour Party had been warmly welcomed by Ben-Gurion; but now Gaitskell forced a vote which the Government won by 270 votes to 218.

Grave Disorder

On November 1st the new Secretary of State for Defence, Anthony Head, made a statement to the House:

"Last night, bombing attacks were made by British aircraft on four Egyptian airfields: Almaza and Inchass, Abu Sueir and Kabrit. First reports show that bombing results were accurate. There was some heavy and light flak but no damage to our aircraft. One aircraft was intercepted by a night fighter, but no damage resulted. Ground attack aircraft, shore and carrier based, carried out attacks on a total of nine Egyptian airfields this morning ....."

Hugh Gaitskell quickly responded: "Is the Minister aware that millions of British people are profoundly shocked and ashamed that British aircraft should be bombing Egypt, not in self-defence, not in collective defence, but in clear defiance of the United Nations Charter ....."

Sidney Silverman, an agile Labour back bencher then raised a Point of Order: "Is there anything that the House of Commons can do at this moment to make certain that those who have taken an oath of allegiance to Her Majesty are not required by that oath to commit murder all over the world?"

The Speaker had to intervene in the uproar that followed: "It would be a very bad thing if we were to enter upon the very serious debate which lies in front of us in an atmosphere of noisy interruption. I do hope that we can conduct ourselves, as this House always does on grave matters, with a proper sense of what is due to Parliament and to the House of Commons."

The Speaker's words were largely ignored and ten minutes later, Hansard noted that: "Grave Disorder having arisen in the House, Mr. Speaker, pursuant to Standing Order Number 24 (Power of Mr. Speaker to adjourn House or suspend Sitting) suspended the Sitting of the House for half an hour." It was the first time that the House had been suspended because of "Grave Disorder" since 1936.

When the House reassembled, the level of acrimony had not diminished. Douglas Jay – Hugh Gaitskell's friend and advisor, was soon asking: "If there has been no actual declaration of war ..... do not these operations amount to an act of organised murder by the British Government?"

Transatlantic Trauma

Just over an hour before the House of Commons had been suspended because of "Grave Disorder", the American National Security Council met at the White House. The Secretary of State opened the discussion. The memorandum of the discussion of the 102nd meeting of the National Security records that:

" ..... Secretary Dulles expressed his view that the British and French would not win. Indeed, recent events are close to marking the death knell for Great Britain and France. These countries have acted deliberately contrary to the clearest advice we could possibly give them. They have acted contrary both to principle and to what was expedient from the point of view of their own interests ..... "

At that meeting, the Anglo-French position was defended by Governor Harold Stassen, a former Governor of Wisconsin who had been talked of as a potential Republican presidential candidate in the 1940s. As a member of President Eisenhower's Cabinet with responsibility for disarmament negotiations, he had recently led an unsuccessful move to replace Richard Nixon as Vice-President.

"Governor Stassen ..... emphasized that the British feel that they cannot possibly have an individual like Nasser holding their lifeline in his hands ..... The British had committed a terrible error. On the other hand, it was a vital friend who had committed this error and our real enemy was the Soviet Union ..... The British ..... were facing a genuine crisis. They had made a judgement that the future of Great Britain depended on getting the Canal into friendly hands again ..... Governor Stassen emphasised that he could not see how it would serve the interests of the United States to strike now at Britain and Israel."

"With great warmth, Secretary Dulles said he was compelled to point out to Governor Stassen that it was the British and French who had just vetoed the proposal for a cease-fire ..... and added that what the British and French had done was nothing but the straight old-fashioned variety of colonialism of the most obvious sort."

"Both Secretary Humphrey (Treasury) and the Attorney General ..... expressed a preference for stopping arms shipments to the whole Near Eastern area. They believed that our action should cover the whole area and not be confined to a single country such as Israel."

"Secretary Dulles, in response, pointed out that we had only yesterday been arguing in the U.N. Security Council in favour of suspending economic and financial assistance to the Israelis. Could we now abruptly change? Mr. Allen Dulles (C.I.A.) pointed out that if the British and French were branded as aggressors, would we not have to apply sanctions against them as well as against Israel. This seemed to Mr. (Allen) Dulles a very dangerous course of action."

" ..... Governor Stassen ..... pointed out that we could not fail to consider the state of mind of the Israelis in the face of so many provocations and fears. Secretary Dulles answered that one thing, at least, was clear: We do not approve of murder. We have simply got to refrain from resort to force in settling international disputes."

"The President expressed agreement with Secretary Dulles's position ..... "

United Protests

In the Foreign Office it had been expected that the United Nations discussion of the fighting in the Middle East would be temporarily halted by the Anglo-French vetoes cast in the Security Council. When the Hungarian crisis had developed in mid-October, however, there had been some conversations between the British and American delegations about reviving the "Uniting for Peace" formula which could be used for transferring a debate from the Security Council to the General Assembly. This procedure had only been used once before in 1950 when South Korea was invaded. Now, the American delegation discussed with the Soviet Union and Yugoslavia the possible use of the "Uniting for Peace" formula to transfer the Middle East debate to the General Assembly. Seven votes were needed in the Security Council to transfer the debate. Ambassador Lodge, the chief American delegate, cast the seventh vote.

After condemning Britain, France and Israel in the National Security Council meeting at the White House, John Foster Dulles flew to New York and immediately addressed the special session of the General Assembly.

After beginning his speech by saying: "I doubt that any representative ever spoke from this rostrum with as heavy a heart as I have brought here tonight", he launched into another bitter attack on his former friends:

"The United Nations may have been somewhat laggard, somewhat impotent, in dealing with many injustices inherent in this Middle Eastern situation. I think that we should, and I hope that we shall, give our most earnest thought – perhaps at the next regular session of the General Assembly – to the problem of how we can do more to establish and implement the principles of justice and international law. We have not done all that we should have done in that respect, and on that account part of the responsibility for the present events lies at our doorstep."

"If, however, we were to agree that the existence in this world of injustices which this Organisation has so far been unable to cure means that the principle of renunciation of force should no longer be respected, that whenever a nation feels that it has been subjected to injustice it should have the right to resort to force in an attempt to correct that injustice, then I fear that we should be tearing this Charter into shreds, that the world would again be a world of anarchy, that the great hopes placed in this Organisation ..... would vanish and that we should again be where we were at the start of the Second World War, with another tragic failure in place of what we had hoped - as we can still hope - would constitute a barrier to the recurrence of world war, which, in the words of the preamble to the Charter, has twice in our lifetime brought untold sorrow to mankind."

Dulles closed his denunciation of the Anglo-French-Israeli action by saying: "It is still possible for the united will of this Organisation to have an impact upon the situation ..... not only for the benefit of ourselves but for all posterity ....." As one country after another denounced Britain, France and

Israel, the only glimmer of light for the British delegation came in the speech of Lester Pearson, the Foreign Minister of Canada, who suggested the formation of a special United Nations force to police the area.

At 2:30 a.m. on November 2nd, the General Assembly voted 64 to 5 in favour of the American Resolution. Australia and New Zealand had voted with Britain, France and Israel. There were 6 abstentions: Belgium, Canada, Laos, The Netherlands, Portugal and South Africa.

The British case had been presented by Sir Pierson Dixon, the British Permanent Representative at the United Nations. When Anthony Eden was Foreign Secretary in 1943, he had appointed young Pierson Dixon as his Principle Private Secretary. In the years that followed they had often worked together. Sir Pierson's judgement carried special weight with the Prime Minister. Sir Pierson now warned that: "our friends are greatly alarmed that we may have to leave the U.N."

The House of Commons met soon after the debate at the United Nations General Assembly had ended. When Hugh Gaitskell asked whether the Prime Minister would accept the resolution calling for a Middle East cease-fire passed by "an overwhelming majority" of the Assembly, the Prime Minister noted that he had not had time to study the resolution or the speeches. It was agreed that the House would – unusually – hold a special session on Saturday, November 3rd. The Cabinet now met at 10 Downing Street. As the Cabinet minutes show, the Foreign Secretary painted a bleak picture:

"..... The Cabinet should take account of the strength of the feelings which the Anglo-French action had aroused in the United States. If no concession were made to those feelings, it was possible that oil sanctions might be imposed against us. We might then be compelled to occupy Kuwait and Qatar, the only suppliers of oil who were not members of the United Nations; and we should alienate, perhaps irretrievably, all the Arab States. The government of Syria had already broken off relations with the United Kingdom. It was possible that Iraq, Jordan and Libya would follow her example. In Iraq this would have disastrous consequences for the Prime Minister would fall and the King himself might be overthrown. We could not hope to avoid serious difficulties with the Arab States for more than a very short time longer, certainly not for as long as it would take us to complete an opposed occupation of Egypt."

R. A. Butler, the Leader of the House, then added a further gloomy note:"The Government's position in the House of Commons ..... was now as favourable as it could be expected to be during the present crisis. This was undoubtedly the result of the Prime Minister's offer to transfer the responsibility for the Suez area to a United Nations force. This Parliamentary position could not be maintained unless the initiative which the Government had established on the previous evening was exploited ....."

After much further discussion the Cabinet decided that: " ..... Our objective should therefore be to establish detachments of Anglo-French forces between the combatants at key positions along the Canal and to make it clear that we should welcome any reinforcement of these detachments which the United Nations could provide. At the same time we should press for some further retirement by the Israeli forces, perhaps to twenty miles, instead of ten miles, from the Canal in order both to demonstrate to the world our impartiality between the two combatants and to reinforce the Government of Iraq in their efforts to maintain political stability in their country and to preserve their connection with the United Kingdom. Any additional requirement of this kind should be put to the Government of Israel before their troops actually reached the Canal."

Mopping up in Sinai

On the afternoon of November 2nd while the British Cabinet was suggesting that the Israeli armed forces should be told not to get within 20 miles of the Canal, Israeli soldiers had nearly completed the occupation of Northern and Central Sinai. Gaza had surrendered on November 2nd while

Israeli armoured columns were approaching the old Suez Canal Company Headquarters at Ismailia. Israeli casualties amounted to 100 killed and 700 wounded. More than 5,000 Egyptian soldiers had been captured. The amount of Soviet equipment captured in the main Egyptian base of El Arish almost equalled the quantity of Israeli tanks and trucks that had broken down during the swift advance across Sinai. One Israeli aircraft was shot down by a British warship on patrol near the Straits of Tiran.

There was one Israeli target left – and this was the most important of them all - the Egyptian batteries that enforced the blockade of the Straits of Tiran. After Nasser had imposed his blockade in October 1955, Ben-Gurion had proposed in the Israeli Cabinet that the Israeli defence forces should capture Sharm el- Sheikh and the neighbouring positions. In November 1955, Ben-Gurion had been prepared to risk diplomatic condemnation and the bombing of Israeli cities in order to break the blockade. His cabinet colleagues rejected this proposal; but, in November 1956, Sharm el-Sheikh was still the major Israeli objective.

After the 64 to 5 hostile vote in the U.N. General Assembly, the French were almost as keen as the Israelis to press ahead quickly. Admiral Barjot, the French Deputy Commander, was told by the French government to try and see that French soldiers landed on Egyptian soil "within two hours". General Ely, the French Chief of Staff, flew to London to argue with the case for a swift strike with the British Chiefs of Staff. Without any prompting from their ministers, the French Commanders on Cyprus were already bombarding General Keightley and his staff with various plans - *Omelette* or *Telescope* - for a quick parachute landing near Port Said.

General Keightley was not impressed with these French arguments. The latest aerial reconnaissance of Port Said and the northern section of the Canal zone showed that there had been a substantial increase in the number of Egyptian soldiers in the area. Many of the Egyptian soldiers had come from the Sinai where President Nasser had ordered a withdrawal against the wishes of his army commander, General Amer. Some of these reinforcements from

69

Sinai had already been defeated in battles with the Israelis; but they still had their weapons and there was no reason to think that they would not use them. After the sharp lesson of Arnhem, where airborne forces had tried to capture "a bridge too far", British military doctrine decreed that after a jump a parachute unit should be supported by tanks as quickly as possible. On November 2nd 1956, the nearest British tanks were on landing craft in the convoy coming from Malta. They were still three days away from the Egyptian coast. November 4th or November 5th was the very earliest day on which Anglo-French forces could land in Egypt.

While General Keightley seemed to be moving slowly, the men of the 3rd Battalion of the Parachute Regiment were preparing to take part in the British Army's first battalion-sized operational drop since the end of World War II. During the summer they had returned to England for a swift parachute jumping refresher course. They would drop on Gamil Airfield to the west of Port Said.

The aged Hastings and Valetta aircraft that would lift 3 Para could not carry the vehicles that 3 Para now used in Cyprus. The Battalion was now issued with ancient jeeps which could be carried. 3 Para also had to hand in their F.N. rifles which were supposed to jam in the sand. They were reissued with the rifles of El Alamein vintage. There were special new wireless sets – which did not survive their parachute drop.

While the men of 3 Para were preparing to draw their parachutes, the 1st and 2nd Battalions of the Parachute Regiment were climbing onto landing craft. The three operational airfields in Cyprus were jammed with more than 250 allied aircraft. Only one British parachute battalion and one French parachute battalion could be lifted at a time; but the decision to send the two remaining British parachute battalions to Egypt by sea meant that the British Headquarters had thrown away its ability to launch further airborne operations down the Canal.

Helping the Burglar

Tempers had not improved when the House met at noon on November 3rd. Hugh Gaitskell opened the debate by saying: "What they have done is to destroy all faith in collective security. What they have done now, by refusing to accept the United Nations Resolution is virtually to destroy that institution, which the Prime Minister once described as the hope of mankind. What we did was to go in and help the burglar and shoot the householder."

The spirit of verbal, hand to hand combat continued through the debate. As Denis Healey said: "At this moment thousands of young Englishmen are sitting in landing craft .... moving towards the shores of Egypt. I spent some time in the last war in exactly that situation ..... The fact is that unless those landing craft are redirected to another destination in the next few hours, thousands of young men may carry on their souls for the rest of their lives, the feeling that they faced personally the same sort of problem as soldiers in the German Army in the last war faced and that they failed to meet it rightly ....."

At that point, Charles Pannell, a Labour M.P., raised a Point of Order: "Is it in order for the Honourable Member of Essex Southeast (Mr. Bernard Braine) to refer to My Honourable Friend as a 'traitorous defeatist'? It was said within the hearing of all of us." After the Deputy Speaker's ruling, the phrase "traitorous defeatist" was withdrawn; but the spirit of acrimony continued in the debate.

As Douglas Dodds-Parker, who was on the Government front bench, recalled: "I sat watching – I could scarcely hear – with fascination as a socialist lady screamed 'You bloody bastards' non-stop for half an hour ..... Little good came out of all this confusion. It could not then stop the action to which we were committed. It only made it harder for those concerned to concentrate on making a success of the dedication of our forces."

On the evening of November 3rd, the Prime Minister addressed the nation on television and radio: "All my life", he said, "I have been a man of peace, working for peace, striving for peace, negotiating for peace. I have been a League of Nations man and a United Nations man and I'm still the same man with the same convictions, the same devotion to peace ..... but I am utterly convinced that the action we have taken is right ..... Between the wars we saw things happening which we felt were adding to the danger of a great world war. Should we have acted swiftly to deal with them, even though it meant the use of force, or should we have hoped for the best and gone on hoping and talking as, in fact, we did? There are times for courage, times for action, and this one of them."

As Leader of the Opposition, Hugh Gaitskell claimed the right of reply. The BBC was reluctant to agree; but Tony Benn, who had become Gaitskell's unofficial broadcasting advisor, now suggested that Gaitskell's office should announce that Gaitskell would be replying. This would force the BBC's hand. The corporation would have to explain why they were not allowing Gaitskell to speak. At the beginning of the Suez crisis, Gaitskell had written in his diary: "Tony Benn ..... although talented in many ways, a good speaker and a man of ideas, had extraordinarily poor judgement." Tony Benn now helped prepare Gaitskell's response to Eden's broadcast: "Make no mistake about it – this is war: the bombing, the softening up, the attacks on radio stations ..... to be followed very, very soon now by the landings and the fighting between ground forces. We are doing all this alone, except for France, opposed by the world, in defiance of the world. It is not a police action, there is no law behind it – we have taken the law into our own hands."

When the Cabinet met at 6:30 p.m. on November 4th it had to decide whether the Anglo-French airborne assault should go forward the following morning. At an earlier meeting, the Chiefs of Staff had sounded an uncertain note. The First Sea Lord seemed to be suggesting that the convoy from Malta should bypass Port Said and sail on instead to Gaza or even to Haifa – a suggestion that raised General Templer's blood pressure to dangerous levels. In the Egypt Committee, which had met earlier in the afternoon, the Foreign Secretary had once again reported the United Nations sanctions might soon become a reality, while an additional problem was created when the Israeli delegation at the United Nations suggested that their country was accepting the call for a cease-fire. This seemed to be unlikely as the Israelis had not yet captured Sharm el-Sheikh.

At the end of the full Cabinet meeting, the Prime Minister asked his colleagues whether they were in favour of going ahead with the military operation, or of postponing it for 24 hours, or for delaying further military action indefinitely. Unusually, a formal vote was taken. Twelve Cabinet Ministers were in favour of going ahead; three (Butler, Kilmuir and Heathcoat Amory) were in favour of postponement and three (Lord Salisbury, Buchan-Hepburn and Monckton) were in favour of stopping altogether.

Fighting in the Streets

At dawn on November 5th, 668 British paratroopers dropped on Gamil Airfield. The landing of British troops did not produce a cease-fire in the House of Commons.

Tony Benn kept the temperature high when he asked: "Will the Foreign Secretary tell the House whether he authorised the broadcast from Cyprus yesterday at 05:45 hours" ..... He then quoted from the text of a message that had been prepared as part of the earlier 'shock and awe' strategy: " 'It means that we are obliged to bomb you wherever you are. Imagine your villages being bombed. Imagine your wives, children, mothers, fathers and grand-fathers escaping from their houses and leaving their property behind. This will happen to you if you hide behind your women in the villages .....

If they do not evacuate there is no doubt that your villages and homes will be destroyed. You have committed a sin – that is, you placed your confidence in Abdul Nasser.' " Tony Benn went on to ask: "In view of the fact that I received this text from the Foreign Office this morning, will the Foreign Secretary take responsibility for it and explain whether it does, in fact, lie behind the policy of Her Majesty's Government?"

Soon after Selwyn Lloyd had said: "I have no knowledge of that broadcast", Nye Bevan joined in the attack by reading out the contents of a leaflet which had supposedly been prepared by the psychological warfare experts in Cyprus: "One thing which you can do is to wear civilian clothes. And go to your homes to see if any soldiers or tanks are concealed in your villages. Tell them to clear out before we come and destroy those villages. If they do not evacuate, there is no doubt that your villages and homes will be destroyed. You have committed a sin, that is, you have placed confidence in Abd Al-Nasir and believed his lies. Now, you are hearing the truth."

While the government was under fire in the House of Commons, the men of 3 Para had consolidated their hold on Gamil Airfield and advanced across a cemetery and a sewage farm towards the streets of Port Said. Twelve men of 3 Para had been injured while defeating the Egyptian company that was guarding the airfield. Across the harbour in Port Fuad, 500 French parachutists had jumped from 400 feet onto a smaller Dropping Zone. The French paratroopers soon consolidated their hold on Port Fuad which normally was the home of a French community of 1,600.

Early in the afternoon of November 5th, the French had made contact with General Moguy, the senior Egyptian officer in Port Said. Brigadier Mervyn "Tubby" Butler, the Commander of 16 Para Brigade, joined in the talks. After some discussion about the surrender of Egyptian forces, a temporary cease-fire was arranged and a report was sent to Headquarters in Cyprus who immediately forwarded the signal to London.

The Prime Minister now rose after Bevan's question about the anti-Nasser pamphlet and told the House: "I have had a flash signal from the Commander in Chief in the eastern Mediterranean which affects the discussion which is now taking place ..... This is the flash signal which is, of course, subject to confirmation: 'Governor and Military Commander, Port Said, now discussing surrender terms with Brigadier Butler. Cease-fire ordered.'"

There was no cease-fire in the House of Commons. The final question of the day was put by John Eden, a Conservative Member who was the nephew of the Prime Minister: "Is the Right Honourable Gentleman aware that the BBC had been broadcasting to the outside world details of the shameful partisan demonstrations sponsored by the Opposition? May I ask the Leader of the Opposition and his Honourable and Right Honourable Friends, whether they wish that Egypt or Britain should win?"

When the Speaker left the Chair, the Times reported that: "Members crowding both sides of the Chamber rose shouting and cheering. As the Prime Minister and the Foreign Secretary made their way from the Chamber, the Conservatives cheered loudly. Labour Members joined in a sustained chorus of boos and shouts which continued for some time."

On Shore – Slowly

When the plans for military intervention had first been discussed in August 1956, General Stockwell, the Land Force Commander designate, had pointed out some of the problems about using Port Said as the main landing place. He had preferred Alexandria. Port Said, General Stockwell had said, was like a cork in a bottle with a very long neck. It was, in fact, an island surrounded by water and marsh; and connected to the Egyptian mainland by a narrow 20 mile causeway. Dock space inside the Port was limited. General Stockwell's assessment was right.

On the afternoon of November 5, the LST carrying 1st Para had completed its 300 mile journey from Cyprus. On some of the battalion wireless sets it was possible to hear a 3 Para signal office urgently calling on their carrier-based air support not to strafe their own forward positions - a message that was expressed in colourful and vigorous language. Meanwhile, fresh orders about naval bombardment had been forwarded from Cyprus: "No gun of greater calibre than 4.5 inches will be fired." In effect, there was to be no bombardment – although naval gunfire support was not prohibited. When the Egyptians opened fire with one of their Soviet SU100 guns at a British destroyer, a returning salvo had set fire to part of the Arab shanty town.

By dawn on November 6th, the huge armada from Malta had arrived at

Port Said. It was expected that the harbour itself had been heavily mined; and mine-clearance diving teams went to work shortly before 0800 hours. After four hours, they could find no mines. The two parachute battalions that had travelled by sea (in an LST and a cross-channel ferry) were supposed to have followed the commandos ashore; but they did not reach their landing place by the Casino Palace Hotel until shortly before 4:00 in the afternoon.

There was, of course, considerable confusion on the streets of Port Said. How many Egyptian troops were there in the city? It seemed probable that there was at least one brigade, but some soldiers were trying to leave. Would the remaining Egyptian soldiers fight or surrender? On the day before the landings, the problem was compounded by the Russian Consul, Anatoly Tchikov, who had spent hours distributing large quantities of Czech rifles and machine guns, that had been stored in local warehouses as part of the Czech arms deal. They were handed to any Port Said resident who would take them. At the same time, he told anyone who cared to listen that World War III was about to start and that the Soviet Union was already bombing London and Paris.

The Italian Consul was more helpful. He provided a refuge in his Consulate for worried Europeans and was also busy trying to arrange a cease-fire. As a result of the Italian Consul's efforts, General Stockwell, accompanied by the Naval and Air Force Commanders, set off in a boat towards Navy House, a robust building which dominated the harbour of Port Said. There they expected that they would receive the surrender of the Egyptian forces. As General Stockwell's boat approached Navy House, there was a burst of machine gun fire that almost hit them. "I don't think they are ready to receive us yet" said Admiral Durnford-Slater. The party quickly retreated towards the de Lesseps statue on the quayside.

A rather similar problem was faced by the first flight of Commandos who were carried into Port Said by helicopter. For several years, Admiral Mountbatten had argued in favour of "vertical envelopment", a new stratagem which involved carrying troops from aircraft carriers into battle by helicopter and landing them at strategic points behind the enemy lines. After considerable argument, the convoy from Malta had included two light carriers, *Theseus* and *Ocean*, which carried 600 Commandos and 24 assault helicopters. Mountbatten's idea of "vertical envelopment" would now be put into practice for the first time. At first, it had been planned that the helicopters should land near a bridge on the main road south from Port Said; then it was decided to land 45 Commando near the city centre. The lead helicopter saw a suitable landing place in a sports arena. The pilot was about to unload his passengers when a burst of machine gun fire nicked the pilot's hand. They had inadvertently landed on an Egyptian strongpoint. The helicopter took off as quickly as it had landed, thus unexpectedly proving that helicopters could carry troops out of battle as well as into battle. The commandos landed safely near the de Lesseps statue.

Navy House was stoutly defended by the Egyptians until the early evening on November 6th despite repeated rocket attacks by the cab-rank of carrier-based aircraft. A huge cloud of black smoke from burning oil tanks at the back of the harbour provided a dramatic backdrop for the confused fighting on the streets of Port Said. The move south down the Canal had barely begun by mid-afternoon.

Stop or Go

At 11:00 a.m. on November 6th, Members of the House of Commons were summoned to the House of Lords to hear the Queen open a new session of Parliament. The Cabinet met at 9:45 a.m., shortly after General Stockwell had turned back from his hazardous trip towards Navy House in Port Said.

The political and diplomatic situation had not improved. Macmillan had received confirmation that the American Secretary of the Treasury, would stop any attempt to strengthen Britain's financial position by blocking help from the International Monetary Fund. The Russians had also found their voice. While Soviet soldiers were completing the forcible destruction of Nagy's government in Budapest, Bulganin had sent hostile messages to the governments of Britain, France and Israel: "We are fully determined to crush the aggressors by the use of force and to restore peace in the East."

Meanwhile, reports from the United Nations building in New York seemed to be almost as threatening as Bulganin's message. After receiving an inaccurate report from United Nations staff in Cairo that British aircraft were bombing the Egyptian capital, the Secretary General's interventions had become even more hostile. In messages sent directly to the Foreign Secretary, Sir Pierson Dixon had to report that there was a grave risk of "collective measures of some kind against Britain and France" unless he could report that all bombing would stop.

The good news from the United Nations was, in its way, almost as disconcerting as the warning messages. Both Israel and Egypt had accepted the Assembly's call for a cease-fire. There was also a strong probability that the Secretary General would be able to announce, within 24 hours, plans for the establishment of a serious United Nations Force. As ministers were constantly pointing out that Britain and France had intervened to separate the combatants, there was now no further political reason for advancing down the Canal.

At the beginning of a Cabinet meeting on November 6th, Selwyn Lloyd argued that: "It was now urgently necessary that we should regain the initiative in bringing hostilities to an end while there was an opportunity to carry with us the more moderate sections of opinion in the General Assembly. It was equally important that we should shape our policy in such a way as to enlist the maximum sympathy and support from the United States government." But as Selwyn Lloyd went on to argue: "A menacing letter had just been received from President Bulganin calling on the United Kingdom to stop the war in Egypt, and stating that the Soviet government was submitting to the United Nations a proposal to employ, together with other members of the United Nations, naval and air forces in order to bring the war in Egypt to an end and to curb aggression. We must not appear to be yielding in the face of

Soviet threats and our reply to the Secretary General of the United Nations must not be such as to give that impression."

In the discussion that followed Selwyn Lloyd's pronouncement it was argued that:"It would still be practicable to proceed with the Anglo-French occupation of the Canal area, regardless of opposition from any quarter. But, if we adopted this course, we must reckon with the possibility of a Soviet invasion of Syria or some other area in the Middle East, and possibly a direct Soviet attack on the Anglo-French forces in the Canal area. It was also probable that the other Arab States in the Middle East would come actively to the aid of Egypt, and that the United Nations would be alienated to the point of imposing collective measures, including oil sanctions, against the French and ourselves."

The decisive voice in arguing for a cease-fire had been that of Harold Macmillan. At the end of October, Macmillan had told the Cabinet about the precarious state of the country's financial reserves. The intensifying financial pressure was an important factor in persuading Macmillan to support a cease-fire. At that time, he was also well aware of another un-recorded and un-minuted reason for stopping. As a former Foreign Secretary, he was particularly conscious of the fact that the decisive 64-to-5 vote in the United Nations General Assembly had made it peculiarly difficult to overthrow Nasser. When the military intervention had first been planned, there was a general assumption that the occupation of the Canal zone would lead to the collapse of Nasser's government. This was clearly now unlikely to happen, while the size of the vote in the General Assembly had put an unavoidable roadblock in the path of any advance towards Cairo. Macmillan recognised that Nasser could not be defeated. Anthony Nutting was referring to the vote in the United Nations General Assembly when he wrote in his biography of Nasser: "From that moment, Nasser could not lose the war even though he was sure to lose every battle."

Of course, it would be possible to occupy the whole of the Canal zone quickly. The ever cautious General Keightley had suggested that this might take six more days, while the French seemed to think that two days would be more than enough. But what good would that be if it was impossible to move against Nasser in Cairo?

In 1956, a British re-occupation of the whole Canal zone would be costly in terms of men and money, and would almost certainly not lead to Nasser's removal. A British battalion in Ismailia would merely provide a target for Egyptian snipers. Nasser would not want to see British and French soldiers on the Canal or Israelis in Sinai; but, with the support of the United States and the Soviet Union and the emerging Afro-Asian bloc, he would be more comfortable politically than his opponents. The United Nations vote had also made him invulnerable to the various schemes for internal upheavals that had been half-heartedly encouraged by British Intelligence.

Shortly before noon on November 6th, a message was sent to Keightley: "It may be essential politically to have an immediate cease-fire and to stand fast. Could you maintain the force, at present ashore indefinitely, from present positions assuming maintenance through Port Said?" After a delay of nearly two hours, Keightley replied: "The answer is 'yes'. Present forward positions midway between Port Said and Qantara." – a rather optimistic assessment.

In Port Said, General Stockwell's Chief of Staff first heard that a cease-fire was imminent from a BBC news broadcast. Communications between the British Headquarters on Cyprus and General Stockwell's Headquarters, on a boat just outside Port Said Harbour, were almost as uncertain as the communication between General Stockwell and the units under his command.

In the late afternoon of November 6th, General Stockwell was preparing his orders for the move south to Qantara and possibly Ismailia on November 7th. Now, there would be no November 7th. The cease-fire order would come into force at 2:00 a.m. Intelligence reports had suggested that the 20 mile causeway linking Port Said with the Egyptian mainland would be heavily defended. In fact, preliminary reconnaissance showed that there were no Egyptian mines or strong points at all on the causeway. In the dark, the lead battalion, 2 Para, dashed down the causeway in a curious collection of vans, taxis and cars that had been "liberated" by Major Anthony Farrar-Hockley, a staff officer at 16 Para Brigade Headquarters who had already distinguished himself in Korea. 2 Para arrived at the end of the causeway, a few minutes after the cease-fire had come into effect at 2:00 a.m. Canal Time.

Clearly, the French would have to be told, if not consulted, and Eden telephoned Guy Mollet saying that the British Cabinet wanted a cease-fire within a few hours. Mollet argued that the operation should continue for two or three more days. At every level, the French were furious. When Admiral Barjot heard of the probable cease-fire while having lunch with General Keightley in Cyprus, he immediately began to plan further operations using the French paratroopers who were ready and waiting on Tyambou airfield. Perhaps a French battalion could be dropped behind the Israeli lines and capture Ismailia. General Beaufre was also thinking of a French advance down the Canal, leaving their British allies behind. In Paris, some of Mollet's Ministers were also in favour of going on without the British. Bourgès-Maunoury, the Minister of Defence, was in favour of continuing alone. The British had been too cautious. Robert Lacoste, the Minister with special responsibility for Algeria, pointed out that millions of Arabs would think that the cease-fire was a victory for Nasser and would be encouraged to intensify the Algerian revolt. After much muttering, Guy Mollet's argument, that the French should agree to Eden's cease-fire, carried the day.

The end of British participation in this brief conflict was announced by the Prime Minister at 6:00 p.m. in the House of Commons. He told Members that as the Secretary General of the United Nations was able to confirm that Egypt and Israel had accepted an unconditional cease-fire and that as a competent international force would soon come into existence, Great Britain would stop further military operations. As he told the House: "If, as a result of the actions we have taken, the United Nations is more ready to employ forces adequate to the duties it has to discharge, the better it will be for the peace and the future of the world."

The Times parliamentary correspondent then noted: "As the Prime Minister resumed his seat there was a great outburst of cheering from his supporters and this spread from the floor of the House to the Member's Galleries above. They jumped up, waving Order papers and handkerchiefs."

Uncomfortable Days

Within 48 hours on the cease-fire, General Stockwell's Chief of Staff was writing: "Tactically, our position could hardly be worse ..... We are deployed on about a one tank front. The main threat we have to meet is air attack against which we have little or no warning or defence ..... A high proportion of the force is loaded in ships, many of which are now on the high seas .....The whole of this situation will produce .....a most ghastly administrative problem."

The British troops on shore were living in some discomfort. 1 Para was deployed on a beach to the west of Port Said which they shared with the ammunition dump of the 6th Royal Tank Regiment, some of whose tanks had travelled up the causeway. A trooper in 6 RTR accidentally started a fire in the dump. The Adjutant of 1 Para bravely ran forward with a fire extinguisher only to be blown head over heels by the force of a major explosion. Miraculously, there were no serious casualties.

Across the harbour in Port Fuad, the French were more comfortable. 24 hours after the cease-fire, an enterprising journalist from the Sunday Times visited the French Headquarters. The house was empty; but in the dining room the table had been prepared for a formal dinner. There were several wine glasses at each place and a small, cold Egyptian chicken on every plate. There were no wine glasses on British tables, although the Household Cavalry's silver had arrived unexpectedly – without the regiment.

There were also continuing tensions in the transatlantic special relationship. On November 6th, Anthony Eden had talked on the telephone to President Eisenhower to tell him of the Anglo-French cease-fire and to congratulate the President on his re-election with a much increased majority. Eden had suggested that they should meet immediately in Washington and for the moment Eisenhower agreed. Within hours, Eisenhower had withdrawn his acceptance of Eden's suggestion. Dulles was in hospital recovering from an operation for colon cancer; but Herbert Hoover Jr. and Ambassador Lodge, strongly advised against such a high level meeting.

On November 12th, Selwyn Lloyd travelled to the United Nations in New York. The day after his arrival, he was invited to dinner by Cabot Lodge. At the end of World War I, the Ambassador's father had led the successful campaign to stop the United States joining the League of Nations. He had been the Senator from Massachusetts where the large Irish-American electorate had traditionally taken a firmly anti-British line. Twenty years later, young Cabot Lodge had taken his father's place in the Senate before becoming his country's Ambassador at the United Nations. At dinner on November 13th, Cabot Lodge's attitude would have pleased the most anti-British of his former constituents. What the British had done was indefensible aggression. The bitter tone of the conversation made it plain that it would be some time before the traditionally easy relationship between the British and American delegations could be restored.

When Selwyn Lloyd visited Foster Dulles in hospital, however, the American Secretary of State asked why the British had not gone on and removed Nasser. Selwyn Lloyd was polite enough not to tell the invalid Secretary of State that the American stratagem of switching the United Nations debate to the General Assembly had provided Nasser with his best defence.

The Conservative Whip's office also faced some uncomfortable moments. Only eight back benchers had abstained in a vote of confidence on November 7th; but as the Chief Whip, Edward Heath, was well aware, there was widespread dismay about the cease-fire. Why had we stopped when we were about to win?

The official explanation that we had succeeded in stopping a small war which, in its turn had stopped a much larger war, did not seem wholly satisfactory.

A more satisfactory explanation was provided by the Chancellor of the Exchequer himself. The Treasury's currency reserves were disappearing. The Sterling Area might break up completely if there was no financial support from America. There was some doubt about the validity of the Treasury's figures for the losses from the reserves; but Macmillan made it plain to anyone who would listen that there would be a financial crisis and an oil crisis if the military operation continued.

On November 9th, Sir Harold Caccia, the new British Ambassador, had presented his credentials to the President who had been re-elected three days before with a majority of 10 million votes. Their conversation had been friendly; but when the new Ambassador had gone on to talk to the American Secretary of the Treasury, George Humphrey borrowed Gaitskell's phraseology and said that; "the United Kingdom is a burglar who has climbed though the window while Nasser is the householder in his nightshirt appealing to the world for protection."

Going to Jamaica

On November 13th, the Prime Minister did not preside over a Cabinet meeting because of his need for rest. It was hardly surprising for Anthony Eden had the most fragile health of any of the main political leaders dealing with the Suez crisis. In September 1955, President Eisenhower had a substantial heart attack just before Nasser announced the Czech arms deal; but he had recovered quickly.

Anthony Eden's health problems, however, were more severe. In 1953, a botched bile duct operation had almost ended his political career. A second operation in Boston had repaired much of the damage, but problems could and did recur. As he described his own problem at the beginning of 1957: "It is now nearly four years since I have had a series of bad abdominal operations which left me with a largely artificial inside. It was not thought that I would lead an active life again. However, with the aid of mild drugs and stimulants I have been able to do so." At the beginning of October 1956, he had been suddenly stuck by a high fever – with a temperature of 106 degrees – while visiting his wife who was temporarily in hospital.

Anthony Eden also faced greater political pressure during the crisis than any of the other national leaders. In Jerusalem, the Israeli Prime Minister received angry messages from Eisenhower but Ben-Gurion was buoyed up by the spectacular victories of the Israeli Army in Sinai. He faced no problems in the Israeli parliament. In Washington, Eisenhower cancelled the last three days of his successful election campaign because of the fighting in Egypt. He spent the time playing bridge in the White House with his 'gang' of special friends. In Cairo, Nasser had faced some discouraging hours before he learned of the vote at the United Nations. He had to argue with his Army Commander when he ordered the remnants of the Egyptian Army to withdraw from Sinai, but after November 2nd, he was able to spend much time publicising his political and diplomatic victory in New York. In Paris, Guy Mollet's only parliamentary problems came from Deputies who complained that the operation was moving too slowly.

At Westminster, however, there was unprecedented parliamentary uproar that broke out whenever the House of Commons met. As Anthony Eden's biographer, Robert Rhodes James, who was present as a Clerk in the House of Commons, observed: "Added to this unpleasant and demoralising situation was the factor of physical and emotional   fatigue. Ministers would go to bed exhausted and wake up without having gained much benefit from the sleep to face the uproar again. It was not surprising that nerves and tempers were affected – indeed, it would have been very surprising if they were not ..... Everyone was in a high state of emotion and the parliamentary atmosphere became poisonously charged. One felt that the House of Commons was close to a collective nervous collapse, so fraught was the temper of the time, and these are not the best circumstances for the calm and deliberate making of vital decisions."

The week after the cease-fire had been particularly frustrating for the Prime Minister who still seemed to believe that the full occupation of the Canal zone would have led to the overthrow of Nasser. Now, instead of having to cope with the problems of victory, the Prime Minister had to deal with the dreary details of defeat. There were depressing arguments about who could clear the blocked Canal and how quickly this vital work would start.

And then there was the attitude of the American government. The American administration would not even discuss vital issues before there was a public commitment for the immediate withdrawal of Anglo-French forces from Port Said.

Depression gnawed at Eden's spirit and his bile duct. On November 18th, Anthony Eden's personal doctor, Sir Horace Evans, said that the Prime Minister must have several weeks of complete rest, preferably in the Caribbean sun. The Edens were lent 'Goldeneye', a house in Jamaica that was owned by Ian Fleming, the creator of the James Bond stories and his wife, Anne, who was a very close friend of Hugh Gaitskell.

The Edens decision to follow the doctor's advice and fly to Jamaica upset many Conservatives. Anne Fleming remarked that: "It would have seemed more patriotic to go to Torquay with a sun lamp." Randolph Churchill wrote a savage article pointing out that during the last war, Hitler had not left his troops at Stalingrad in order to fly to Jamaica. Randolph Churchill was an old critic of the Prime Minister and his savage remark was never forgiven; but many loyal members of the Conservative Party now wondered whether Anthony Eden could survive for long as Prime Minister.

Eden's departure meant that he was not present at the crucial cabinet meetings on November 27th and November 28th which discussed the withdrawal of the Anglo-French force from Port Said. As Macmillan argued, American help was essential and: "this good will could not be obtained without an immediate and unconditional undertaking to withdraw the Anglo-French force from Port Said."

Macmillan's argument did not win universal support in the Cabinet. If the Prime Minister had been present, there can be little doubt that he would have argued strongly against his Chancellor's proposal. Eden believed that the Anglo-French presence in Port Said was: "a gage of importance." Macmillan did not believe that this gage had any value. The closure of the Canal meant that the Egyptian government lost some revenue. The cost to the British government through the disruption of oil supplies was much greater. It was important that the clearance of the Canal should begin as quickly as possible. This could not happen until the Anglo-French force had withdrawn. And if there was going to be a satisfactory discussion about the long term management of the Canal, it was essential to have American support. In the absence of the Prime Minister, the Chancellor of the Exchequer carried the day. The gage would be discarded.

On December 3rd, Selwyn Lloyd made the announcement in the House of Commons: "We have stopped a small war and prevented a large one. The force which we temporarily interposed between the combatants is now to be relieved by an international force …..Responsibility for securing a settlement of the long term problems of the area has now been placed squarely on the shoulders of the United Nations." It was not a day that Conservative Members wished to remember.

There was some compensation. At last, the American response was positive. The scale of American help, once an unconditional withdrawal was announced, had been discussed at the National Security Council meeting on November 9th. The American oil companies would be told to move quickly. They did. Within three days of Selwyn Lloyd's announcement, oil shipment across the Atlantic reached 200,000 barrels a day. The American Export-Import bank announced that a loan of 500 million dollars would be made available on easy terms and the International Monetary Fund approved a British drawing of 561 million dollars. Doing what the President wanted did have its rewards.

Eden Returns and Departs

On December 14th, Eden flew back to London. As Clarissa Eden wrote in her diary:" ..... returned to find everyone looking at us with thoughtful eyes." The Cabinet had vetoed the draft of a statement that the Prime Minister had wanted to make at the airport.

The morale of the Conservative Party was low. Many of those who enthusiastically supported armed intervention were depressed by the way in which it had ended; and there were continuing prods from the Opposition front bench about collusion.

On December 20th, the Prime Minister referred to Suez when replying to the Christmas adjournment debate:"I want to say this on the question of foreknowledge and to say it quite bluntly to the House that there was not foreknowledge that Israel would attack Egypt – there was not. But there was something else.There was – we knew it perfectly well – a risk of it and, in the event of the risk of it, certain discussions and conversations took place ..... I would be compelled ..... if I had the same very disagreeable decisions to take again, to repeat them." Those words were the last that Anthony Eden spoke in the House of Commons. They provided an unhappy close to an unhappy year in Parliament.

During the Christmas recess at Chequers, the fevers and sleepless nights returned. Sir Horace Evans went down to examine his distinguished patient. There were other specialist opinions; their unanimous verdict was straightforward:"The Prime Minister's health gives cause for anxiety. In spite of the improvement which followed his rest before Christmas, there have been a recurrence of abdominal symptoms. This gives us much concern because of the serious operation in 1953 and some subsequent attacks of fever. In our opinion, his health will no longer enable him to sustain the heavy burdens inseparable from the office of Prime Minister."

Eden resigned on January 8th. The persistent bursts of fever that followed his resignation gave ample proof that the doctors' verdict was right. Among the messages that he had received on his retirement there was an invitation to stay from Sidney Holland, the Prime Minister of New Zealand. On January 18ᵗʰ, the Edens sailed to New Zealand through the Panama Canal on *R.M.S. Rangitata.* Their cabin steward was John Prescott, who won the regular ship's boxing competitions so often that he was given a special prize, a bottle of wine, by the former Prime Minister.

While sitting in his cabin, Eden had ample opportunity to think about the tactics and the strategy of Suez. As he wrote to Selwyn Lloyd, even with hindsight he did not think, "that some other course had been possible." He went on to tell Selwyn Lloyd: " ..... I have only one prayer, that you will support the Israelis in their demand for freedom of passage for all commerce in the Gulf of Aqaba." While Eden wanted to back the Israelis, President Eisenhower was threatening to impose economic sanctions unless the Israelis withdrew quickly and completely.

Support for the Israeli position did represent a change from Eden's earlier attitude. At the beginning of August, days after Nasser had nationalised the Canal Company, Eden had been insistent that Macmillan's proposal (supported by Churchill) for getting the Israelis "to make faces" at the Egyptians should not even be discussed by the Cabinet. If Eden had then encouraged the Israelis to break the illegal blockade of the Gulf of Aqaba and to defeat the Egyptian Army in Sinai, Nasser might well have been removed. The Israelis, it seemed, were willing to move independently. British and French forces might then have reoccupied the Canal zone with little opposition.

In the same letter to Selwyn Lloyd, Eden noted that: "Clarissa and I had a small bet anonymously on a horse in one of our ship's games. I couldn't resist it. '*No Policy*' by Eisenhower out of Dulles, and it won. I swear I had nothing to do with the christening or anything else." It was hardly surprising that Eden should be thinking about American policy. If only Eden had insisted that armed intervention should not begin until the week after the American presidential election, President Eisenhower's reaction might not have been so fierce. Even if the British and French had decided to move just before the presidential election, some of the savage American opposition might have been avoided if Macmillan had been sent across the Atlantic to talk to the President.

In fact, the American intervention had been decisive. The American President had stabbed the British Prime Minister in the front.

There was no suggestion that Eden had changed his view about the implacable hostility of Nasser. As he wrote to the formidable Irene Ward before sailing: "I find it strange that so few, if any, have compared these events to 1936 – yet it is so like. Of course, Egypt is no Germany, but Russia is, and Egypt just her pawn. If we had let events drift until the spring, I have little doubt that by then, or about then, Russia and Egypt would have been ready to pounce, with Israel as the apparent target and Western interests as the real one. Russians don't give away all that equipment for fun. Yet so many fail to see this and give Nasser almost as much trust as others gave Hitler years ago."

During the long years of retirement that followed his political death, Anthony Eden was comforted by his firm belief that he had been right.

It's Macmillan!

On January 10th 1957, Harold Macmillan became Prime Minister. Unusually, he had been chosen after a vote of all the members of the Cabinet. The only Cabinet Minister who voted for Rab Butler was Patrick Buchan Hepburn, whose Beckenham constituency was next to Harold Macmillan's Bromley seat. Patrick Buchan Hepburn soon disappeared unto the House of Lords.

It had been generally expected that Rab Butler would succeed; but during the whole Suez crisis, Rab Butler had seemed to dither while Macmillan had always seemed decisive, although sometimes in opposite directions – "First in, first out". At a time when Conservative Party morale was low, Harold Macmillan had the ability to raise Party morale while Rab Butler, a born administrator, could rarely lift his audience's spirits.

There was one other indirect benefit that flowed from the choice of Harold Macmillan – although it probably did not affect the vote of any of his Cabinet colleagues. Macmillan was a friend of President Eisenhower who immediately sent him a note of congratulation which ended with the words: " ….. Remember the old adage, 'now abideth faith, hope and charity – and greater than these is a sense of humour.'" Their friendship went back to 1943 when Macmillan's first important political appointment had been as the British Minister resident at General Eisenhower's Headquarters in North Africa.

In January 1957, the Anglo-American relationship did not arouse much merriment; but it was soon arranged that the Prime Minister and the President should meet in Bermuda, a choice of site which allowed the Prime Minister to welcome the President onto British territory.

After their first informal conversation, Macmillan noted that Eisenhower: "….. talked very freely to me – just exactly as in the old days. There were no reproaches – on either side; but (what was more important) no note of any change in our friendship or the confidence he had in me. Indeed, he seemed delighted to have somebody to talk to! In America, he is half King, half Prime Minister. This means that he is rather a lonely figure. He told me very frankly that he knew how unpopular Foster Dulles was with our people and with a lot of his people. But he must keep him. He couldn't do without him ….."

Near the end of the meeting, Macmillan reported to Rab Butler in London: "First, we have not been in the dock. On the contrary, the Americans have been rather apologetic about their position. Secondly, the personal relations between myself and the President have been established upon a level of confidence which is very gratifying ….. The test, of course, will be how far this spirit will in fact permeate the complicated machinery of Washington departments."

The Bermuda Conference led immediately to the stationing of 60 Thor intermediate range ballistic missiles in Great Britain with a 'dual key' provision – the rockets could not be launched without the approval of both the British and the American governments. The agreements reached at the Bermuda Conference would lead to much closer technical defence co-operation and there was an understanding that the McMahon Act would soon be repealed. This Act, passed in 1946, had prevented the American government from sharing any nuclear knowledge with any other country. Its abolition later in 1957 substantially increased the scope of Anglo-American technical defence co-operation.

Even before Bermuda, President Eisenhower had changed the thrust of American policy in the Middle East. Vice President Nixon later told Julian Amery, the Suez sceptic, that President Eisenhower had come to believe that his Suez policy had been the biggest mistake made while he was in the White House. Some support for this admission is provided by the President's proposals for an 'Eisenhower Doctrine' which would give the American President increased powers to intervene militarily in the Middle East without having to seek Congressional approval. The President had launched his new policy at a four-hour meeting with Congressional leaders on New Year's Day, 1957. This doctrine was supposed to fill the presumed vacuum that would follow from the presumed decline of British and French capabilities in the Middle East.

The first person to ask for direct American help was President Chamoun, the Christian pro-Western leader of Lebanon. When faced with internal political problems, he twice asked for America to intervene. President Eisenhower alerted the U.S. Sixth Fleet in the Mediterranean, but these crises passed before direct intervention was needed. Then, in July 1958, the Iraqi Royal Family and their Prime Minister, Nuri es-Said, were murdered in a left-wing coup. The President of Lebanon and the King of Jordan both asked for British and American help. President Eisenhower and Prime Minister Macmillan carefully co-ordinated their plans.

Days later, American Marines stormed across the beaches of Beirut while bathing holiday makers looked on in surprise. In a parallel operation, two British battalions were flown from Cyprus to Jordan. As Macmillan said to Eisenhower on the telephone: "You are doing a Suez on me." This time it worked.

We Like Ike

On August 27 1979, Harold Macmillan met President Eisenhower's plane at Heathrow. It was Eisenhower's first visit to England since the end of World War II. The seventeen mile journey from the airport to the centre of London took two hours because of the size of the cheering crowds. The Prime Minister was surprised by the warmth of the greeting and the size of the crowds. No foreign leader had ever received such a warm welcome to London.

Before the President's arrival, there had been a flicker of anxiety that there might be some anti-American demonstration during the President's visit. When the Suez crisis had been at its height, the President had received a number of critical letters from his wartime colleagues such as General Ismay and Lord Tedder, reproving him for turning against his wartime allies. As far as the general public was concerned, however, the anti-Americanism that flourished in the aftermath of Suez had all been focused on John Foster Dulles. President Eisenhower's role remained publicly invisible.

During his visit, the President made a joint television appearance with Harold Macmillan in which they stressed the warmth and the strength of the Anglo-American alliance. A general election was imminent and Herbert Morrison noted sourly that all this: "..... offered wonderful election propaganda on the eve of the announcement of the polling date." The American administration was well aware of this; but as the American Secretary of State had noted: "we don't want to see Bevan win".

In 1956, the government's Suez policy had provoked reactions of unprecedented violence. The rancorous scenes in the House of Commons were reflected throughout the country. The storm, however, had subsided almost as quickly as it had arisen. As that eminent psephologist, David Butler pointed out in his study of the 1959 General Election: "the biggest difference between the parties - their attitude towards Suez - was rarely brought up. The Conservatives ignored it because it had caused internal Party strife; Labour was hesitant to stress the issue for fear that its criticisms made it seem unpatriotic." David Butler noted that 67% of Labour candidates had mentioned Suez in their election addresses but there was only a passing reference to Suez in the Labour Party's five television programs.

Anthony Eden took little part in the election campaign. He sent messages supporting the Conservative Party; but he pointedly did not publicly praise his successor. Eden felt that Harold Macmillan had got too close too quickly to the American administration. Three years later, President Eisenhower's stab in the front still hurt.

When the votes were counted, the Conservatives had increased their majority in the House in the Commons from 67 to 107. It seems probable that memories of the conflict helped the Conservatives.

If Suez had become an election issue, the Prime Minister could have pointed out that the outcome of the dispute had done remarkably little damage to British interests. Psychologically, Britain's arraignment at the United Nations and the slow march to Port Said had left numerous scars; but, in practice, very little had altered. Appropriately, the first government department to feel the post-Suez wind of change was the Ministry of Defence. The Anglo-French expeditionary force had not lost a single skirmish; but it had clearly been unsuccessful. While Eden and Mollet were obsessed with their memories of pre-war appeasement, the British planners remembered too well their battles in World War II. It was time for a change. When he was the Chancellor of the Exchequer before Suez, Harold Macmillan had wanted to reduce the defence estimates by cutting back on Fighter Command. After Suez, he installed Duncan Sandys to reshape Great Britain's defence structure. National Service would soon be abolished.

Even after Duncan Sandys' restructuring, however, Great Britain was still a power of the first rank. The testing of a hydrogen bomb had confirmed Great Britain's military status; and diplomatically Great Britain still had a permanent place on the Security Council – although this might have been lost if an Anglo-French force had tried to capture Cairo in 1956. Clearly, British forces would be unlikely to move again in direct opposition to the policies of the United States of America and the Soviet Union; but in 1959, Great Britain still possessed a considerable base in Aden and would soon take strong independent military action to protect its dominant interest in Kuwait. In the early 1950's Great Britain had given Sudan full independence without taking proper steps to provide a better balance between the Islamic/Arab north and the Christian/Animist black south. Millions died in the Sudanese civil war that followed. This issue might have been handled with greater sensitivity if Sudanese independence had not become a major factor in the Suez argument. Elsewhere, in Africa or the Far East, the Suez controversy had minimal direct or indirect impact on the pace of decolonisation.

Keith Kyle has given his splendid history of Suez the sub-title 'Britain's End of Empire in the Middle East'; others might argue that Britain's Empire in the Middle East had ended on July 1954 when Anthony Eden had announced that the British garrison in the Canal zone would soon be withdrawn and that there would be "a new pattern of friendship" in the Middle East. Almost exactly two years later, the future Duke of Norfolk became the last British soldier in the last British battalion to leave the Canal zone.

Three Years Later

While the British voters were busy re-electing their Conservative government, the other main actors in the Suez drama were facing variable political fortunes in 1959. In Washington, President Eisenhower was contemplating retirement to his Gettysburg farm.

In Israel, Ben-Gurion had reinforced his position as the father of his country. Israel's swift victory in Sinai had enhanced the prestige of its armed forces, while the success of General Dayan gave Israel a new hero who was instantly recognisable. The deployment of the U.N.E.F. helped to give Israel ten years of peace before its spectacular success in the Six Day War.

In Egypt, Nasser's political and diplomatic victory at the United Nations completely obliterated memories of his military defeat in the Sinai. Within Egypt his position was totally secure; but his hopes of creating an Arab Empire in his own image were beginning to crumble. Political union with Syria proved to be unexpectedly difficult; and the temptation to meddle in the Yemen soon became fatally attractive. The Iraqi coup of July 1958 looked as though it was another Nasserite success; but the new Iraqi leaders soon proved that they were marching to a different tune. The presence of the U.N.E.F. meant that Nasser did not have to rush into another confrontation with Israel; but, sooner or later, his pride would make him try to avenge the Egyptian military humiliations of 1948 and 1956. In 1959, when Nasserism still looked like the wave of the present and the future, very few Middle Eastern experts would have predicted that almost 50 years later, Jordan, Saudi Arabia and the members of the United Arab Emirates would still be dominated by their traditional ruling families.

In France, Guy Mollet's government had taken the lead in calling for military action against Nasser. It had also been the first to suffer. The French soldiers who returned to Algeria from Port Said felt that they had been betrayed by their political masters, while the Algerian rebels took fresh heart. The 4th Republic was replaced by President De Gaulle and Algerie Française soon died. Guy Mollet had also been a keen advocate of the new European Economic Community. Memories of Suez undoubtedly increased the satisfaction that President de Gaulle felt when he vetoed Macmillan's application for British membership of the E.E.C.

Fifty Years On

In 1956, Anthony Eden was prepared to cut some ethical corners because he believed that President Nasser's policies were a direct threat to the economic survival of his country. Eden was prepared to put at risk his political life by going to war without the approval of the United Nations. Eden's policy momentarily divided the nation; but, three years later after his own political death, the uproar had been largely forgotten.

Almost fifty years later, Anthony Blair was prepared to cut some ethical corners because he fervently believed that Saddam Hussein's Iraqi government was a threat to peace and stability in the Middle East. He was prepared to go to war without the approval of the United Nations. Blair's policy provoked some opposition within his own party and his own cabinet, although it never generated the domestic uproar that had greeted Anthony Eden's actions. Three years later, however, Anthony Blair's ethical corner-cutting still generates muttering at home and there is still violence in Iraq.